Math
Activity Book

4

Book Staff and Contributors

Lisa White *Lead Content Specialist*
Megan Simmons *Content Specialist*
Lauralyn Vaughn *Manager, Instructional Design*
Susan Raley *Text Editor*
Tricia Battipede *Senior Creative Manager*
Jayoung Cho *Senior Visual Designer*
Caitlin Gildrien *Visual Designer*
Tricia Battipede, Mike Bohman, Shannon Palmer *Cover Designers*
Deborah Benton, Dana Crisafulli, Michele Patrick, Maureen Steddin, Alisa Steel, David Stienecker *Writers*
Amy Eward *Senior Manager, Writers and Editors*
Abhilasha Parakh *Senior Project Manager*

Doug McCollum *Senior Vice President, Product Development*
Kristin Morrison *Vice President, Design, Creative, and UX*
Rohit Lakhani *Vice President, Program Management and Operations*
Kelly Engel *Senior Director, Curriculum*
Christopher Frescholtz *Senior Director, Program Management*
Erica Castle *Director, Creative Services*
Lisa Dimaio Iekel *Senior Production Manager*

Illustrations Credits

All illustrations © Stride, Inc. unless otherwise noted
Characters: Tommy DiGiovanni, Matt Fedor, Ben Gamache, Shannon Palmer
Cover: Bird © Mara008/Shutterstock; Pastel wallpaper patterns © mxtama/iStock.
Interior Pattern: Pastel wallpaper patterns © mxtama/iStock.

At Stride, Inc. (NYSE: LRN)—formerly K12 Inc.—we are reimagining lifelong learning as a rich, deeply personal experience that prepares learners for tomorrow. Since its inception, Stride has been committed to removing barriers that impact academic equity and to providing high-quality education for anyone—particularly those in underserved communities. The company has transformed the teaching and learning experience for millions of people by providing innovative, high-quality, tech-enabled education solutions, curriculum, and programs directly to students, schools, the military, and enterprises in primary, secondary, and post-secondary settings. Stride is a premier provider of K-12 education for students, schools, and districts, including career learning services through middle and high school curriculum. Providing a solution to the widening skills gap in the workplace and student loan crisis, Stride equips students with real world skills for in-demand jobs with career learning. For adult learners, Stride delivers professional skills training in healthcare and technology, as well as staffing and talent development for Fortune 500 companies. Stride has delivered millions of courses over the past decade and serves learners in all 50 states and more than 100 countries. The company is a proud sponsor of the Future of School, a nonprofit organization dedicated to closing the gap between the pace of technology and the pace of change in education. More information can be found at stridelearning.com, K12.com, destinationsacademy.com, galvanize.com, techelevator.com, and medcerts.com.

ISBN: 978-1-60153-577-1

Printed by Walsworth, Saint Joseph, MI, USA, March 2021.

Table of Contents

Equivalent Fractions and Comparison

Angles and Their Measurements

Adding and Subtracting Fractions and Mixed Numbers

Multiplication by a 1-Digit Number

Multiplication by Two 2-Digit Numbers

Division by a 1-Digit Divisor Without Remainders

Measurement Units

Problem Solving Involving Measurements

Comparing with Multiplication and Division (A)

Practice Comparing with Multiplication

Write an equation for the comparison statement.

1. Five times as much as 7 is 35.

   $7 \times \boxed{5} = 35$

2. Six times as much as 3 is 18.

   $6 \times 3 = 18$

3. Three more than 7 is 10.

   $3 \times 7 = 10$

4. Twenty-eight is 7 times as much as 4.

   $4 \times 7 = 28$

Write a comparison statement for the equation.

5. $7 \times 9 = 63$

   $9 \times 7 = 63$

I am 3 times as old as my little brother!

Solve.

6. The tape diagram models the number 3.

$$\boxed{3}$$

   a. Draw a tape diagram that models 5 times as much as 3.

   b. What is 5 times as much as 3? _____

7. Marla swam 7 laps in a pool. Zahara swam 3 times as many laps as Marla. Let n represent the number of laps Zahara swam.

   a. Write an equation to solve for the number of laps Zahara swam.

   _____

   b. Solve for n.

   $n = \boxed{}$

   c. Complete the sentence.

   Zahara swam $\boxed{}$ laps.

8. What is 6 times as much as 8? _____

9. Kenji's sister is 6 years old. Kenji is 4 times as old as his sister. How old is Kenji? Write your answer in a complete sentence.

   _____

Comparing with Multiplication and Division (B)

Practice Comparing with Division

Solve.

1. Francesca filled 20 pails of water, which is 4 times the number of pails that Caitlin filled.

   a. Circle 4 equal groups of pails.

   b. How many pails are in one of the equal groups? _____5_____

   c. How many pails did Caitlin fill? Write your answer in a complete sentence.

   _____

2. Latasha is 40 years old, which is 8 times as old as Nadir. Let n represent Nadir's age. How old is Nadir?

   a. Complete the equation that can be used to solve this problem.

   $n =$ [5]

   b. Find Nadir's age.

   _____5_____

3. Malik owns 24 hats. Amir owns 4 hats.

   a. Circle as many equal groups of 4 hats as possible.

   b. How many groups of 4 hats are in 24 hats? _____

   c. How many times as many hats does Malik own as Amir? Write your answer in a complete sentence.

   _____

4. Angelo has 63 marbles, which is 7 times as many marbles as Jonah has. Let *m* represent the number of marbles Jonah has. How many marbles does Jonah have?

   a. Complete the equation that can be used to solve this problem.

   $m = $ [   ]

   b. Find the number of marbles Jonah has.

   _____

5. Paula has $48 in her piggy bank, which is 6 times as much money as Danika has in her piggy bank.

   How much money does Danika have in her piggy bank? _____

Multiples and Factors (A)

Practice Working with Shape Patterns

Write the rule for the pattern. Then, write a sentence that describes a feature of the pattern.

1. ♥ ■ ■ ♥ ■ ■ ♥ ■ ■

   Rule: heart, square, _square_

   Feature: Two squares are always between two hearts.

2. ★ ● ☾ ★ ● ☾ ★ ● ☾

   Rule: _star circle moon_

   Feature: _a circle is always to the left of a moon_

3. ▲▲ ▬ ● ▲▲ ▬ ● ▲▲ ▬ ●

   Rule: _triangle triange rectangle circle_

   Feature: _a rectangle is always between a circle and triangle_

4. ♥ ★ ♥ ☾ ♥ ★ ♥ ☾ ♥ ★ ♥ ☾

   Rule: _heart star heart moon_

   Feature: _a heart is always next to the moon_

Complete the pattern.

5. ● ● ● ▲ ● ● ▲ ● ● ▲ _○_ _○_ _△_

6. ▲♥■ ■▲♥ ■■▲ ♥■■ _△_ _♡_ _▢_

7. ● ■ ★ ● ■ ■ ★ ● ■ ★ ● _▢_ _★_ _○_ _■_ _★_

8. ☾▲● ●☾☾▲● ●☾☾▲● ●☾☾▲● _☾_ _☾_ _▲_ _○_ _☾_

Draw the pattern from the given rule. Repeat the rule at least three times in your drawing.

9. rectangle, triangle, circle

10. circle, triangle, triangle, square

Create a pattern of your own. Write the rule for the pattern. Then, draw the pattern so that it repeats the rule at least three times.

11. Rule: _Star star heart triangle_

   Pattern: _☆ ☆ ♡ △ ☆ ☆ ♡ △ ☆ ☆ ♡ △_

Multiples and Factors (B)

Practice Working with Numbers in Patterns and Equations

Write the rule for the pattern.

1. 1, 3, 5, 7 _9_

2. 21, 18, 15, 12 _4_

3. 27, 9, 3, 1 _0_

Find the missing numbers in the pattern.

4.

+4   +4   +4   +4   +4

5,   9,   13,   17,   [21],   [25]

5. 13, 18, 23, 28, _33_, _38_, _43_

6. 4, 10, 16, 22, _28_, 34, _40_, 46, _52_

7. 92, 82, 72, 62, _52_, _42_, 32, _22_

Complete the table.

8.

2	3	4	5
4	6	8	10
6	9	12	15
8	12	16	20

1
2
3
4

9.

1	5	9	13
4	9	14	19
7	13	19	25
10	17	24	31

9
5
6
7

List one feature of the pattern that is not described by the pattern's rule.

10. 4, 9, 14, 19; Rule: Add 5.

Feature: _____

_____

11. 4, 16, 64, 256; Rule: Multiply by 4.

Feature: _____

_____

A feature of this pattern is that the ones digit is always 5. Explain why this pattern has this feature.

12. 15, 35, 55, 75; Rule: Add 20.

_____

_____

_____

Write the first five numbers in the pattern.

13. Starting value: 5

Rule: Add 4.

_____

14. Starting value: 34

Rule: Subtract 2.

_____

Multiples and Factors (C)

Practice Working with Multiples and Factors

Write all of the whole-number factor pairs for the given number.

1. 14 _____

2. 16 _____

3. 6 _____

4. 20 _____

Write the first six multiples of the given number.

5. 4 _____

6. 7 _____

7. 8 _____

8. 10 _____

Write all of the whole numbers that the given number is
a multiple of.

9. 18 _____

10. 12 _____

11. 25 _____

12. 15 _____

Tell whether the sentence is true. Write True or False. Justify your answer.

13. 72 is a multiple of 8.

_____

_____

14. 42 is a multiple of 5.

_____

_____

15. 50 is a multiple of 8.

_____

_____

16. 48 is a multiple of 6.

_____

_____

Wow! Factors and multiples are really connected.

Multiples and Factors (D)

Practice Working with Prime and Composite Numbers

Answer the questions about the given number.

1. 8

   a. What are the factors of 8? _____

   b. How many factors does 8 have? _____

   c. Is 8 prime, composite, or neither? _____

2. 17

   a. What are the factors of 17? _____

   b. How many factors does 17 have? _____

   c. Is 17 prime, composite, or neither? _____

3. 1

   a. What are the factors of 1? _____

   b. How many factors does 1 have? _____

   c. Is 1 prime, composite, or neither? _____

Prime? Composite? Neither? Just look at the factors to figure it out.

Classify the number as prime, composite, or neither.

4. 25 _____

5. 29 _____

6. 42 _____

7. 49 _____

8. 61 _____

9. 9 _____

10. 57 _____

Solve.

11. Kiki states that 2 is composite because it's an even number. Is her reasoning correct or incorrect? Explain.

_____

_____

_____

12. Evan states that 21 is prime because it's an odd number. Is his reasoning correct or incorrect? Explain.

_____

_____

_____

Comparing with Larger Numbers (A)

Practice Reading and Writing Larger Numbers

Follow the steps to write the number name for the number.

1. 34,294

   a. Write the digits of the number in the place value chart.

Millions				Thousands				Ones		
hundred millions	ten millions	millions		hundred thousands	ten thousands	thousands		hundreds	tens	ones
			,				,			

   b. Write the number name.

   _____

2. 320,945

   a. Write the digits of the number in the place value chart.

Millions				Thousands				Ones		
hundred millions	ten millions	millions		hundred thousands	ten thousands	thousands		hundreds	tens	ones
			,				,			

   b. Write the number name.

   _____

Write the number name.

3. 84,307 _____

4. 126,495 _____

Write the standard form of the number.

5. two hundred forty-three thousand, six hundred fifty-four _____

6. eighty-three thousand, twenty-six _____

7. seven thousand, four hundred three _____

8. five hundred six thousand, nine _____

Write the expanded form of the number.

9. 4,609 _____

10. 12,437 _____

11. 829,394 _____

12. 403,282 _____

Write the standard form of the number.

13. 5,000 + 300 + 6 _____

14. 20,000 + 5,000 + 50 + 2 _____

15. 400,000 + 30,000 + 8,000 + 200 + 4 _____

16. 600,000 + 40,000 + 8 _____

Comparing with Larger Numbers (B)

Practice Comparing Larger Numbers

Write the digits of the given numbers into the stated rows of the place value chart. Then, compare the numbers.

1. 4,302 and 4,158

   a. **Row 1:** 4,302; **Row 2:** 4,158

Millions			Thousands			Ones		
hundred millions	ten millions	millions	hundred thousands	ten thousands	thousands	hundreds	tens	ones
Row 1			,			4	,	3	0	2
Row 2			,				,			

   b. Compare the numbers using <, >, or =.

   4,302 ☐ 4,158

2. 56,394 and 56,810

   a. **Row 1:** 56,394; **Row 2:** 56,810

Millions			Thousands			Ones		
hundred millions	ten millions	millions	hundred thousands	ten thousands	thousands	hundreds	tens	ones
Row 1			,				,			
Row 2			,				,			

   b. Compare the numbers using <, >, or =.

   56,394 ☐ 56,810

Compare the numbers using <, >, or =.

3. 34,382 ☐ 34,329

4. 5,493 ☐ 5,519

5. 185,302 ☐ 183,791

6. 83,283 ☐ 9,392

7. 43,396 ☐ 433,963

8. 624,537 ☐ 625,123

9. 62,504 ☐ 62,054

Tell whether the comparison statement is true. Write True or False. Explain your answer.

10. 125,384 > 125,512

_____

_____

_____

11. 78,366 > 76,945

_____

_____

_____

Solve.

12. A zoo has two elephants named Jasmine and Ella. Jasmine weighs 6,832 pounds. Ella weighs 6,732 pounds.

   a. Compare 6,832 and 6,732 using <, >, or =.

   _____

   b. Which elephant weighs more? _____

Multiplying a Fraction by a Whole Number (A)

Practice Using Models to Multiply a Fraction by a Whole Number

Represent the fraction as the product of a unit fraction and a whole number.

1. $\frac{3}{5}$

    a. Draw a model for $\frac{3}{5}$.

    b. Draw a model for $\frac{1}{5}$.

    c. Model the product.

2. $\frac{5}{2}$

Write the equation that the model represents.

3.   =

_____

4.   =

_____

Write an equation to show the fraction as the product of a whole number and a unit fraction.

5. $\frac{5}{6}$ _____

6. $\frac{15}{100}$ _____

7. $\frac{3}{5}$ _____

8. $\frac{18}{5}$ _____

9. $\frac{11}{2}$ _____

10. $\frac{1}{4}$ _____

Solve.

11. Explain how to write $\frac{13}{5}$ as the product of a unit fraction and a whole number.

_____

_____

_____

_____

12. Li drew this model to show $\frac{7}{3}$ as the product of a unit fraction and a whole number.

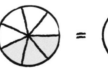

Is Li's model correct? Explain.

_____

_____

_____

_____

Multiplying a Fraction by a Whole Number (B)

Practice Multiplying a Unit Fraction by a Whole Number

Multiply.

1. $4 \times \frac{1}{5}$

    a. Write 4 as a fraction.

$$4 = \frac{\Box}{\Box}$$

    b. Write the new expression.

$$\frac{\Box}{\Box} \times \frac{1}{5}$$

    c. Multiply the numerators and the denominators to find the product. _____

2. $2 \times \frac{1}{3}$ _____

3. $5 \times \frac{1}{100}$ _____

4. $\frac{1}{8} \times 7$ _____

5. $2 \times \frac{1}{6}$ _____

6. $\frac{1}{10} \times 18$ _____

7. $\frac{1}{5} \times 1$ _____

8. $15 \times \frac{1}{2}$ _____

9. $\frac{1}{4} \times 9$ _____

Solve.

10. Alexa and Peter both multiply $\frac{1}{6} \times 7$. Their work is shown.

Alexa	Peter
$\frac{1}{6} \times 7 = \frac{1}{6} \times \frac{7}{1} = \frac{7}{6}$	$\frac{1}{6} \times 7 = \frac{1}{6} \times \frac{1}{7} = \frac{1}{42}$

    a. Who solves the problem correctly? _____

    b. What does the person who solves it incorrectly do wrong?

    _____

    _____

11. Explain how to find the product of a whole number and a unit fraction.

_____

_____

_____

12. How can you find the product $1 \times \frac{1}{8}$ using mental math?

_____

_____

_____

Hooray!
You did it!

Multiplying a Fraction by a Whole Number (C)

Practice Multiplying a Non-Unit Fraction by a Whole Number

Find the product.

1. $6 \times \frac{2}{3}$

     a. Write 6 as a fraction.

$$6 = \frac{\square}{\square}$$

     b. Write the new expression.

     c. Multiply the numerators and the denominators to find the product. _____

2. $6 \times \frac{3}{5}$ _____

3. $11 \times \frac{5}{100}$ _____

4. $\frac{7}{8} \times 5$ _____

5. $2 \times \frac{5}{12}$ _____

6. $\frac{7}{10} \times 2$ _____

7. $\frac{55}{100} \times 1$ _____

8. $9 \times \frac{9}{10}$ _____

9. $\frac{3}{5} \times 2$ _____

10. $\frac{2}{5} \times 0$ _____

11. $2 \times \frac{2}{3}$ _____

Find the unknown number.

12. $10 \times \dfrac{3}{\square} = \dfrac{30}{8}$

13. $\square \times \dfrac{4}{5} = \dfrac{20}{5}$

14. $21 \times \dfrac{\square}{100} = \dfrac{42}{100}$

15. $1 \times \dfrac{\square}{\square} = \dfrac{7}{12}$

Solve.

16. Circle the products that are greater than 1.

$3 \times \dfrac{1}{2}$ $\qquad$ $\dfrac{2}{10} \times 4$ $\qquad$ $31 \times \dfrac{2}{100}$ $\qquad$ $5 \times \dfrac{3}{8}$ $\qquad$ $\dfrac{2}{3} \times 4$

17. Jorge says that $6 \times \dfrac{3}{4}$ is $\dfrac{3}{24}$.

   a. Is Jorge's answer reasonable? Explain.

   _____

   b. What mistake could Jorge have made?

   _____

   _____

   c. What is $6 \times \dfrac{3}{4}$? _____

18. Explain why the product of $8 \times \dfrac{2}{5}$ is equal to the product of $\dfrac{2}{5} \times 8$.

   _____

   _____

Fractions Greater Than One (A)

Practice Writing Improper Fractions and Mixed Numbers

Write the improper fraction as a mixed number.

1. $\frac{13}{5}$

    a. What fraction represents the shaded area of each circle? Write the missing numbers in the boxes.

$$\frac{\square}{5} \qquad \frac{\square}{5} \qquad \frac{\square}{5}$$

    b. Write the missing numbers in the boxes to show the mixed number.

$$\frac{13}{5} = \frac{\square}{5} + \frac{\square}{5} + \frac{\square}{5}$$

$$= \square + \square + \frac{\square}{5}$$

$$= \square + \frac{\square}{5}$$

$$= \square\frac{\square}{5}$$

Write the improper fraction as a mixed number.

2. $\frac{7}{3}$ _____

3. $\frac{9}{5}$ _____

4. $\frac{19}{12}$ _____

5. $\frac{15}{4}$ _____

6. $\frac{13}{2}$ _____

7. $\frac{44}{10}$ _____

8. $\frac{11}{8}$ _____

9. $\frac{45}{6}$ _____

10. $\frac{15}{5}$ _____

11. $\frac{243}{100}$ _____

Write the mixed number as an improper fraction.

12. $10\frac{1}{2}$ _____   13. $4\frac{2}{3}$ _____

14. $1\frac{7}{10}$ _____   15. $9\frac{1}{6}$ _____

16. $8\frac{3}{4}$ _____   17. $3\frac{2}{100}$ _____

18. $4\frac{5}{12}$ _____   19. $5\frac{5}{6}$ _____

20. $2\frac{7}{10}$ _____   21. $11\frac{4}{5}$ _____

Solve.

22. Sarah writes $\frac{19}{4}$ as a mixed number. Her work is shown.

19 fourths = 16 fourths + 3 fourths

$\qquad$ = 3 wholes + 3 fourths

$\qquad$ = $3\frac{3}{4}$

What mistake does Sarah make?

_____

_____

Hmm . . . what went wrong?

Fractions Greater Than One (B)

Practice Solving Problems with Fractions Greater Than One

Solve.

1. A pizza shop uses $\frac{1}{4}$ cup of basil for each pizza. How much basil does it need for 25 pizzas?

   a. Write an expression that can be used to find the amount of basil that is needed for 25 pizzas.

   _____

   b. How much basil is needed? Write your answer as an improper fraction.

   _____

   c. How much basil is needed? Write your answer as a mixed number.

   _____

   d. Between what two whole numbers does your answer lie?

   _____

2. Sonya is cooking chili for a party. The recipe she uses calls for $\frac{3}{4}$ cup of beans. She wants to make 6 times the amount of chili that the recipe makes. How many cups of beans will she need? Write your answer as a mixed number.

   _____

3. For the past 2 nights, Kyle read $\frac{5}{12}$ of his novel each night. Did Kyle read the entire novel during those 2 nights? Explain.

   _____

4. Melanie has 12 cups of broth. She wants to use $\frac{1}{2}$ of it in the soup she is making. How many cups of the broth does she use in the soup?

_____

5. A pack of peanuts weighs $\frac{1}{8}$ pound. How much do 7 packs of peanuts weigh?

_____

6. Jenny walks $\frac{8}{10}$ of a kilometer each day. How far does she walk in 7 days? Write your answer as a mixed number.

_____

7. Danny is $\frac{2}{3}$ as tall as his older sister. His sister is 5 feet tall. How tall is Danny? Write your answer as a mixed number.

_____

8. Rosa practices piano for 25 minutes. She spends $\frac{1}{4}$ of that time practicing scales. How much time does she spend practicing scales? Write your answer as a mixed number.

_____

I am $4\frac{1}{4}$ feet tall!

Equivalent Fractions Concepts (A)

Practice Modeling Equivalent Fractions

Answer the questions.

1. Casey and Dana each order the same small pizza. Casey has a pizza with 4 equal slices, and she eats $\frac{1}{4}$ of her pizza. Dana has a pizza with 8 equal slices, and she eats $\frac{2}{8}$ of her pizza.

    a. Draw a diagram to model how much of the pizza each girl eats.

    b. Do they eat the same number of slices? Explain.

    _____

    _____

    c. Do they eat the same amount of pizza? Explain.

    _____

    _____

    _____

    d. How can they eat the same amount of pizza if they do **not** eat the same number of slices of pizza? Explain.

    _____

    _____

    _____

Shade the model to show an equivalent fraction. Then, write your answer in the box to write the equivalent fraction.

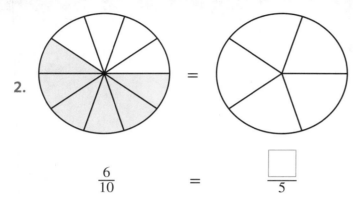

2.

$$\frac{6}{10} = \frac{\boxed{}}{5}$$

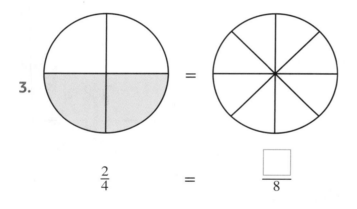

3.

$$\frac{2}{4} = \frac{\boxed{}}{8}$$

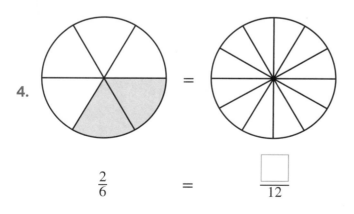

4.

$$\frac{2}{6} = \frac{\boxed{}}{12}$$

Equivalent Fractions Concepts (B)

Practice Explaining Equivalent Fractions

Use the models to answer the questions.

1.   Circle A   Circle B

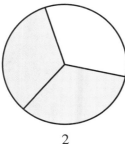 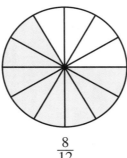

$\frac{2}{3}$ $\frac{8}{12}$

    a. How many total parts is Circle A divided into? _____

    b. How many total parts is Circle B divided into? _____

    c. How many parts are shaded in Circle A? _____

    d. How many parts are shaded in Circle B? _____

    e. How many times greater is the number of total parts in Circle B

        than in Circle A? _____

    f. How many times greater is the number of shaded parts in Circle B

        than in Circle A? _____

    g. Write an equation that shows that $\frac{2}{3}$ is equivalent to $\frac{8}{12}$.

        _____

Shade the models to represent the fractions. Then, use the models to write an equation that shows the fractions are equivalent.

2. $\frac{1}{4}$ and $\frac{2}{8}$

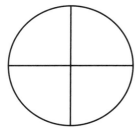 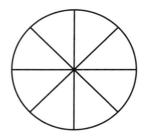

3. $\frac{1}{2}$ and $\frac{6}{12}$

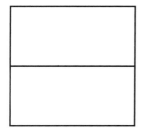 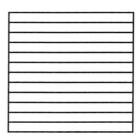

4. $\frac{2}{5}$ and $\frac{4}{10}$

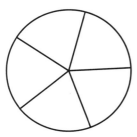 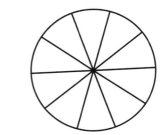

Equivalent Fractions Concepts (C)

Practice Identifying Equivalent Fractions

Answer the questions.

1. Is $\frac{1}{2}$ equivalent to $\frac{5}{10}$?

   a. What number do you multiply 1 by to get 5? _____

   b. What number do you multiply 2 by to get 10? _____

   c. Are the numbers in Part (a) and Part (b) the same number? _____

   d. Are the fractions equivalent? Explain how you know.

   _____

   _____

   _____

Circle the two fractions that are equivalent.

2. $\frac{1}{2}$ $\frac{2}{3}$ $\frac{8}{4}$ $\frac{6}{12}$

3. $\frac{5}{8}$ $\frac{3}{4}$ $\frac{4}{12}$ $\frac{1}{3}$

4. $\frac{5}{6}$ $\frac{2}{3}$ $\frac{8}{12}$ $\frac{2}{6}$

5. $\frac{1}{5}$ $\frac{4}{5}$ $\frac{6}{10}$ $\frac{8}{10}$

6. $\frac{10}{100}$ $\frac{1}{10}$ $\frac{10}{10}$ $\frac{5}{100}$

7. $\frac{1}{2}$ $\frac{2}{6}$ $\frac{2}{3}$ $\frac{4}{6}$

8. $\frac{6}{8}$ $\frac{8}{6}$ $\frac{3}{4}$ $\frac{2}{3}$

Answer the question.

9. Why is $\frac{2}{8}$ equivalent to $\frac{1}{4}$? Draw a model to justify your answer.

_____

_____

_____

Equivalent fractions look different, but they are really the same amount.

Creating Equivalent Fractions (A)

Practice Finding Equivalent Fractions Using Multiplication

Solve.

1. Write two fractions equivalent to $\frac{3}{4}$.

   a. Multiply the numerator and denominator by 2.

   $$\frac{3}{4} = \frac{3 \times 2}{4 \times 2} = \frac{\boxed{}}{\boxed{}}$$

   b. Multiply the numerator and denominator by 3.

   $$\frac{3}{4} = \frac{3 \times 3}{4 \times 3} = \frac{\boxed{}}{\boxed{}}$$

2. Explain why $\frac{10}{100}$ is equivalent to $\frac{1}{10}$.

   _____

   _____

   _____

   _____

Tell whether the fractions are equivalent. Answer Yes or No.

3. $\frac{1}{2}$ and $\frac{5}{10}$ _____

4. $\frac{2}{3}$ and $\frac{4}{6}$ _____

5. $\frac{1}{4}$ and $\frac{3}{8}$ _____

6. $\frac{2}{4}$ and $\frac{6}{12}$ _____

7. $\frac{3}{6}$ and $\frac{5}{12}$ _____

8. $\frac{1}{3}$ and $\frac{3}{6}$ _____

9. $\frac{6}{10}$ and $\frac{60}{100}$ _____

10. $\frac{3}{5}$ and $\frac{6}{10}$ _____

Write two equivalent fractions.

11. $\frac{1}{3}$ _____

12. $\frac{1}{5}$ _____

13. $\frac{2}{4}$ _____

14. $\frac{2}{3}$ _____

Solve.

15. Jemma and Kate each make a blueberry pie like the one shown.

Each girl eats 3 pieces of her pie. Jemma says she ate $\frac{1}{2}$ of her pie.

Kate says she ate $\frac{3}{6}$ of her pie.

Write an equation to show that each girl eats the same amount of her pie.

_____

Creating Equivalent Fractions (B)

Practice Simplifying Fractions

Solve.

1. Write two fractions equivalent to $\frac{8}{12}$.

   a. List the factors of 8. _____

   b. List the factors of 12. _____

   c. List the factors other than 1 that are common to 8 and 12. _____

   d. Divide the numerator and denominator by the common factor 2.

   $$\frac{8}{12} = \frac{8 \div 2}{12 \div 2} = \frac{\boxed{}}{\boxed{}}$$

   e. Divide the numerator and denominator by the common factor 4.

   $$\frac{8}{12} = \frac{8 \div 4}{12 \div 4} = \frac{\boxed{}}{\boxed{}}$$

2. Explain why $\frac{10}{100}$ is **not** in simplest form.

   _____

   _____

   _____

   _____

**Tell whether the fraction is in simplest form. Answer Yes or No.
If the fraction is not in simplest form, write it in simplest form.**

3. $\frac{1}{3}$ _____

4. $\frac{2}{3}$ _____

5. $\frac{5}{10}$ _____

6. $\frac{8}{10}$ _____

7. $\frac{5}{12}$ _____

8. $\frac{7}{8}$ _____

9. $\frac{6}{8}$ _____

10. $\frac{3}{5}$ _____

Write the fraction in simplest form.

11. $\frac{4}{6}$ _____

12. $\frac{6}{10}$ _____

13. $\frac{4}{8}$ _____

14. $\frac{9}{12}$ _____

Solve.

15. Julio eats 4 slices of this pizza. Write the fraction of the pizza he eats in simplest form.

_____

Comparing Fractions (A)

Practice Comparing Fractions Using Models

Compare the fractions using <, >, or =. Use the models to help you.

1. $\frac{4}{5}$ and $\frac{2}{3}$

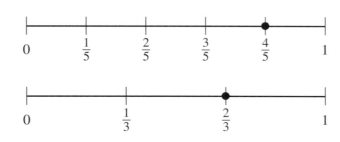

a. As you move right on a number line, do the numbers increase in value or do they decrease in value?

_____

b. Which fraction, $\frac{4}{5}$ or $\frac{2}{3}$, is farther from 0 on the number line? _____

c. $\frac{4}{5}$ ☐ $\frac{2}{3}$

2. $\frac{1}{2}$ ☐ $\frac{5}{12}$

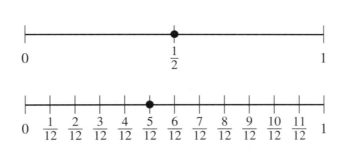

Number lines help me compare fractions!

3. $\frac{3}{5}$ ☐ $\frac{8}{10}$

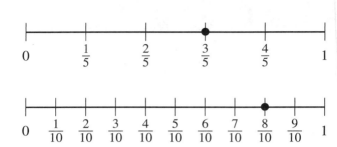

4. $\frac{3}{8}$ ☐ $\frac{7}{12}$

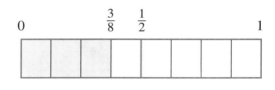

5. $\frac{6}{10}$ ☐ $\frac{2}{4}$

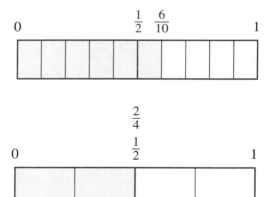

Comparing Fractions (B)

Practice Comparing Fractions Using Common Denominators

Solve.

1. Compare $\frac{2}{3}$ and $\frac{1}{4}$.

   a. Write the first five multiples of 3. _____

   b. Write the first five multiples of 4. _____

   c. What is the least common denominator (LCD) of $\frac{2}{3}$ and $\frac{1}{4}$? _____

   d. Write equivalent fractions using the LCD.

   $\frac{2}{3} = \dfrac{\boxed{}}{\boxed{}}$ $\frac{1}{4} = \dfrac{\boxed{}}{\boxed{}}$

   e. Compare the fractions using <, >, or =.

   $\frac{2}{3} \boxed{} \frac{1}{4}$

Write the LCD of the fractions.

2. $\frac{2}{4}$ and $\frac{5}{8}$ _____

3. $\frac{6}{10}$ and $\frac{65}{100}$ _____

4. $\frac{2}{3}$ and $\frac{3}{4}$ _____

5. $\frac{4}{6}$ and $\frac{11}{12}$ _____

Write equivalent fractions with a common denominator.

6. $\frac{1}{3}$ and $\frac{1}{2}$ using the denominator 12 _____

7. $\frac{3}{4}$ and $\frac{5}{8}$ using the denominator 8 _____

8. $\frac{1}{3}$ and $\frac{1}{2}$ using their LCD _____

9. $\frac{4}{5}$ and $\frac{5}{10}$ using the denominator 10 _____

10. $\frac{4}{8}$ and $\frac{3}{4}$ using the denominator 8 _____

11. $\frac{1}{2}$ and $\frac{2}{4}$ using the denominator 4 _____

Compare the fractions using <, >, or =.

12. $\frac{2}{3}$ ☐ $\frac{1}{2}$

13. $\frac{5}{8}$ ☐ $\frac{3}{4}$

14. $\frac{7}{12}$ ☐ $\frac{2}{3}$

15. $\frac{4}{8}$ ☐ $\frac{6}{12}$

16. $\frac{25}{100}$ ☐ $\frac{2}{10}$

17. $\frac{2}{3}$ ☐ $\frac{5}{6}$

Solve.

18. Cleo buys $\frac{2}{4}$ pound of turkey. Tyler buys $\frac{1}{2}$ pound of turkey.

    Who buys more turkey? Explain.

    _____

    _____

    _____

    _____

Practice Comparing Fractions Using Common Numerators

Solve.

1. Compare $\frac{1}{2}$ and $\frac{2}{3}$.

   a. What is the least common multiple of 1 and 2? _____

   b. Write equivalent fractions with the numerator 2.

   $\frac{1}{2} = \dfrac{\boxed{}}{\boxed{}}$ $\frac{2}{3} = \dfrac{\boxed{}}{\boxed{}}$

   c. Compare the fractions using <, >, or =.

   $\frac{1}{2} \,\boxed{}\, \frac{2}{3}$

Write equivalent fractions with a common numerator.

2. $\frac{1}{3}$ and $\frac{2}{4}$ using the numerator 2 _____

3. $\frac{2}{5}$ and $\frac{4}{12}$ using the numerator 4 _____

4. $\frac{3}{6}$ and $\frac{2}{4}$ using the numerator 6 _____

5. $\frac{2}{4}$ and $\frac{3}{5}$ using the numerator 6 _____

6. $\frac{1}{3}$ and $\frac{4}{5}$ using the numerator 4 _____

7. $\frac{2}{4}$ and $\frac{6}{8}$ using the numerator 6 _____

Compare the fractions using <, >, or =.

8. $\dfrac{1}{3}$ ☐ $\dfrac{2}{5}$

9. $\dfrac{3}{4}$ ☐ $\dfrac{6}{8}$

10. $\dfrac{2}{12}$ ☐ $\dfrac{1}{5}$

11. $\dfrac{4}{8}$ ☐ $\dfrac{2}{5}$

12. $\dfrac{4}{100}$ ☐ $\dfrac{2}{5}$

13. $\dfrac{2}{3}$ ☐ $\dfrac{4}{6}$

Solve.

14. Kay walks $\dfrac{2}{4}$ mile. James walks $\dfrac{3}{5}$ mile. Who walks the greater distance? Explain.

_____

_____

_____

_____

Drawing a picture can be helpful when comparing fractions.

Comparing Fractions (D)

Practice Explaining When It Makes Sense to Compare Fractions

Solve.

1. A rectangle is divided into 5 equal parts with 3 parts shaded. Another rectangle is divided into 10 equal parts with 6 parts shaded. Anthony says that the shaded areas of the rectangles are equal because $\frac{3}{5} = \frac{6}{10}$.

   a. Draw 2 rectangles that could be used to show that Anthony's statement is true.

   b. Draw 2 rectangles that could be used to show that Anthony's statement is **not** true.

   c. What must be true for Anthony's statement to be true?

   _____

   _____

   _____

2. Janelle says that the shaded area of Circle A is greater than the shaded area of Circle B because $\frac{3}{4} > \frac{5}{8}$. Is Janelle correct? Explain.

Circle A

Circle B

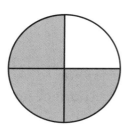

_____

_____

_____

_____

_____

Remember to only compare fractions that represent the same whole!

Concepts of Angle Size (A)

Practice Working with Geometric Objects

Sketch the figure.

1. ray

2. line segment

3. angle

4. line

Sketch the angle.

5. obtuse angle

6. right angle

7. acute angle

State whether each angle in the figure is acute, right, or obtuse.

8.

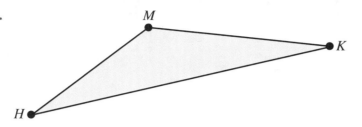

a. angle *H*: _____

b. angle *M*: _____

c. angle *K*: _____

9.

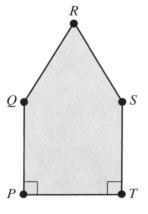

a. angle *P*: _____

b. angle *Q*: _____

c. angle *R*: _____

d. angle *S*: _____

e. angle *T*: _____

Do you think they call them acute angles because they are so cute?

Concepts of Angle Size (B)

Practice Describing Angle Measurements

Use the circle to sketch the described angle. Let the center of the circle be the angle's vertex.

1. straight angle

2. reflex angle

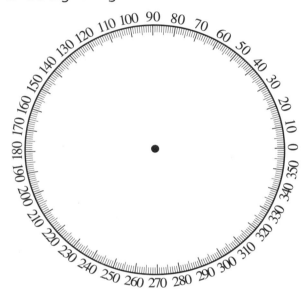
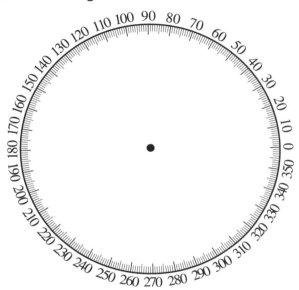

Solve.

3. How many one-degree turns must an angle go through to complete

    a full turn around a circle? _____

4. What fraction of a circle is a one-degree turn? _____

5. An angle has a measure of 48°. How many one-degree turns did

    the angle turn through? _____

Refer to the figure to solve.

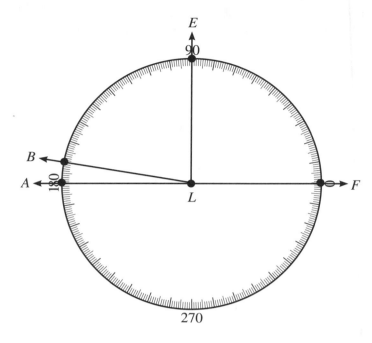

6. Is the angle acute, right, obtuse, straight, or reflex?

    a. angle *ALB*: _____

    b. angle *ALE*: _____

    c. angle *ALF*: _____

    d. angle *BLF*: _____

7. Which angle has an estimated measure of 10°? _____

Concepts of Angle Size (C)

Practice Measuring Angles

Use a protractor to find the measure of the angle.

1.

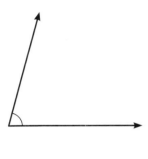

_____

2.

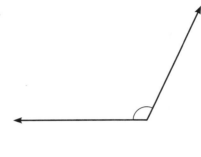

_____

3.

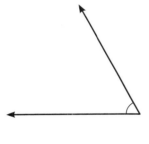

_____

4.

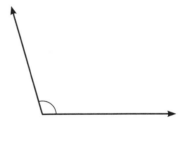

_____

5.

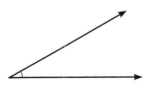

_____

6.

_____

7.

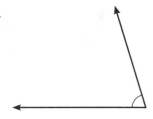

_____

8.

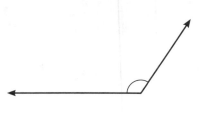

_____

Use a protractor to solve.

9. A ladder leans against a wall. What is the measure of angle *C*, the angle formed by the ladder and the ground?

_____

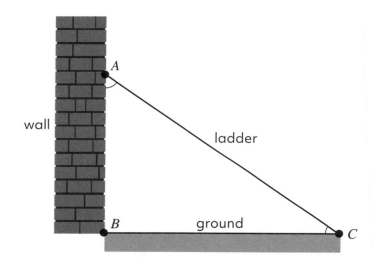

10. What is the measure of angle *A* in this hexagon? _____

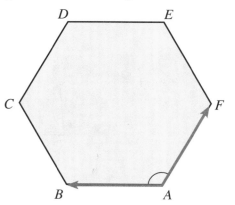

Concepts of Angle Size (D)

Practice Drawing Angles

Use a protractor and the given ray to draw an angle with the given measure.

1. 80°

2. 130°

3. 65°

4. 103°

5. 55°

6. 145°

7. 72°

8. 100°

9. 28°

10. 170°

Calculating with Angles (A)

Practice Calculating with Angles

Solve.

1.

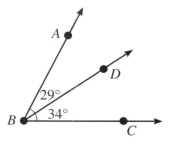

    a. Explain how to solve for the measure of angle ABC.

    _____

    _____

    b. What is the measure of angle ABC? measure of angle $ABC =$ _____

2.

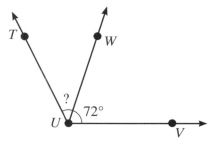

    measure of angle $TUV = 116°$

    a. Explain how to solve for the measure of angle TUW.

    _____

    _____

    _____

    b. What is the measure of angle TUW? measure of angle $TUW =$ _____

Solve for the measure of the named angle.

3.

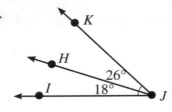

measure of angle $IJK =$ _____

4.

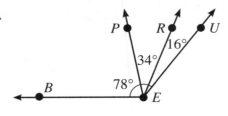

measure of angle $BEU =$ _____

5.

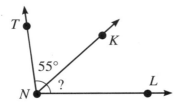

measure of angle $TNL = 98°$

measure of angle $LNK =$ _____

6.

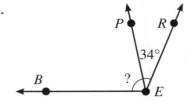

measure of angle $BER = 112°$

measure of angle $BEP =$ _____

Solve.

7. Natalie states that the measure of angle RSV plus the measure of angle TSU equals the measure of angle RST. Is she correct or incorrect? Explain.

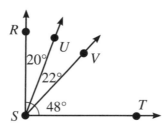

_____

_____

_____

_____

_____

_____

Calculating with Angles (B)

Practice Calculating Angle Measurements in the Real World

Solve.

1. Two of the tiles used in a mosaic are quadrilaterals. One tile has an angle that measures 40°. The other tile has an angle that measures 60°. Together, these two angles form angle ABC.

   What is the measure of angle ABC? _____

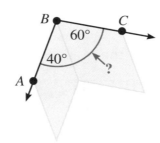

2. A ramp leads to a platform. The ramp forms a 75° angle with the leg of the platform. The platform forms a 90° angle with the leg.

   What is the measure of the angle formed by the ramp and the platform? _____

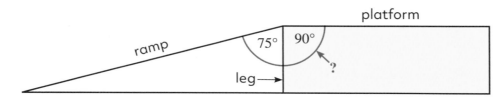

3. An oven door is opened at a 15° angle. It is then opened some more so that it is opened at a 63° angle.

   How many more degrees is the door opened? _____

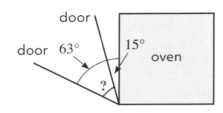

4. The frame of a mirror is made up of 8 wooden pieces. The angle formed by 2 wooden pieces has a measure of 120°. The angle measure of one of the pieces is 60°.

   What is the measure of the angle of the other piece of wood? _____

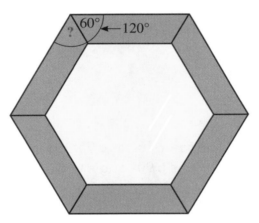

5. While exercising, Rami lifts his arms 35°, 30°, and then 36°.

   What angle does his arm form with his body after the third lift?

   _____

Adding and Subtracting Fractions (A)

Practice Representing Fractions and Mixed Numbers as Sums

Solve.

1. Represent $\frac{2}{3}$ as a sum of fractions with a denominator of 3.

   a. Draw a model that represents $\frac{2}{3}$ as a sum of fractions with a denominator of 3.

   b. Write an equation that represents $\frac{2}{3}$ as a sum of fractions with

   a denominator of 3. _____

2. Draw two different models that represent $\frac{4}{6}$ as a sum of fractions with a denominator of 6.

3. Write an equation that represents $\frac{5}{10}$ as a sum of fractions with

   a denominator of 10. _____

4. Write **all** possible equations that represent $\frac{4}{12}$ as a sum of fractions with a denominator of 12.

_____

_____

_____

_____

5. Write an equation that represents $2\frac{3}{8}$ as a sum of fractions with a denominator of 8.

_____

_____

_____

6. Write two equations that represent $4\frac{1}{2}$ as a sum of fractions with a denominator of 2.

_____

_____

_____

7. Write two equations that represent $\frac{6}{100}$ as a sum of fractions with a denominator of 100.

_____

_____

_____

Adding and Subtracting Fractions (B)

Practice Using Models to Add Fractions and Mixed Numbers

Use the model to find the sum.

1. $\frac{2}{10} + \frac{5}{10}$

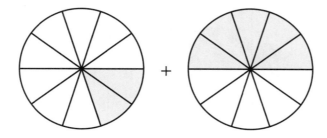

a. Draw a model that puts all the shaded parts together in one circle.

b. How many parts are shaded in your model? _____

c. How many equal parts does your model have? _____

d. What is the sum? _____

2. $\frac{2}{12} + \frac{9}{12}$ _____

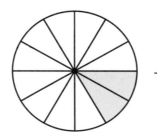

3. $\dfrac{2}{6} + \dfrac{2}{6}$ _____

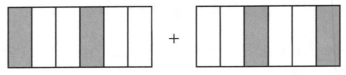

4. $2\dfrac{3}{4} + \dfrac{1}{4}$ _____

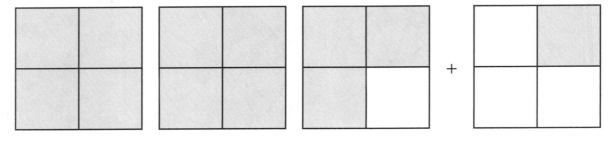

5. $1\dfrac{6}{10} + 1\dfrac{7}{10}$ _____

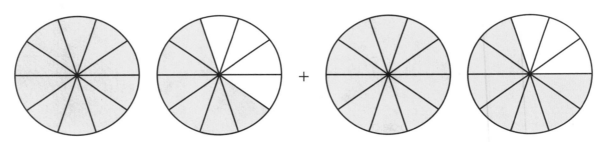

Models help me understand
how to add fractions.

Adding and Subtracting Fractions (C)

Practice Using Models to Subtract Fractions and Mixed Numbers

Use the model to find the difference. Mark the parts that are subtracted with an X.

1. $\frac{7}{8} - \frac{2}{8}$

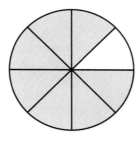

    a. Mark 2 parts with an X to show that $\frac{2}{8}$ are subtracted from $\frac{7}{8}$.

    b. How many parts remain shaded in the model? _____

    c. How many equal parts does the model have? _____

    d. What is the difference? _____

2. $\frac{5}{6} - \frac{3}{6}$ _____

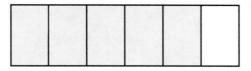

3. $1\frac{5}{12} - \frac{6}{12}$ _____

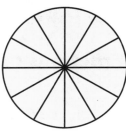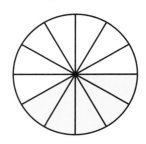

4. $2\frac{3}{4} - 1\frac{1}{4}$ _____

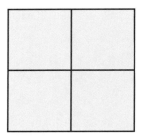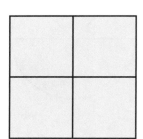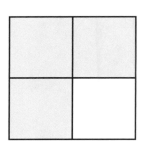

5. $3\frac{2}{5} - 1\frac{4}{5}$ _____

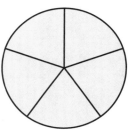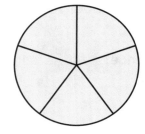

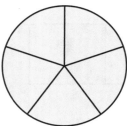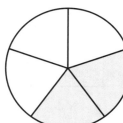

Adding and Subtracting Fractions (D)

Practice Adding and Subtracting Fractions

Solve.

1. Ross adds $\frac{2}{6} + \frac{5}{6}$. He says the sum is $\frac{7}{12}$.

   a. Why is Ross incorrect?

   _____

   _____

   b. What is the correct sum? Write your answer as a mixed number in simplest form.

   _____

Find the sum or difference. Write your answer in simplest form. Convert improper fractions to mixed numbers.

2. $\frac{3}{6} + \frac{2}{6}$ _____

3. $\frac{6}{10} - \frac{3}{10}$ _____

4. $\frac{4}{8} + \frac{2}{8}$ _____

5. $\frac{2}{3} + \frac{1}{3}$ _____

6. $\frac{7}{8} - \frac{4}{8}$ _____

7. $\frac{6}{8} - \frac{5}{8}$ _____

8. $\frac{11}{12} + \frac{9}{12}$ _____

9. $\frac{5}{10} + \frac{2}{10}$ _____

10. $\frac{1}{2} - \frac{1}{2}$ _____

11. $\frac{4}{5} + \frac{3}{5}$ _____

12. $\frac{5}{100} + \frac{2}{100}$ _____

13. $\frac{4}{6} - \frac{3}{6}$ _____

14. $\frac{7}{12} - \frac{4}{12}$ _____

15. $\frac{1}{4} + \frac{1}{4}$ _____

Adding Mixed Numbers (A)

Practice Adding Mixed Numbers Without Regrouping

Find the sum. Write your answer in simplest form.

1. $9\frac{2}{10} + 2\frac{4}{10}$

   a. Add the fraction parts of the mixed numbers and simplify.

   $\frac{2}{10} + \frac{4}{10} = $ _____

   b. Add the whole number parts of the mixed numbers.

   $9 + 2 = $ _____

   c. What is the sum in simplest form?

   $9\frac{2}{10} + 2\frac{4}{10} = $ _____

2. $4\frac{2}{12} + 1\frac{9}{12}$ _____

3. $20\frac{5}{100} + 30\frac{2}{100}$ _____

4. $\begin{array}{r} 8\frac{2}{8} \\ + 3\frac{2}{8} \\ \hline \end{array}$

5. $\begin{array}{r} 7\frac{2}{5} \\ + 9\frac{1}{5} \\ \hline \end{array}$

6. $9\frac{2}{10} + 4\frac{3}{10}$ _____

7. $1\frac{2}{6} + 3\frac{3}{6}$ _____

8. $\begin{array}{r} \frac{4}{8} \\ + 8\frac{2}{8} \\ \hline \end{array}$

9. $\begin{array}{r} 15\frac{2}{12} \\ + 4\frac{3}{12} \\ \hline \end{array}$

10. $4\frac{1}{2} + 3\frac{1}{2}$ _____

11. $5\frac{1}{3} + 2\frac{1}{3}$ _____

12. $\begin{array}{r} 3\frac{4}{100} \\ + 11\frac{6}{100} \\ \hline \end{array}$

13. $\begin{array}{r} 21\frac{1}{4} \\ + 25\frac{2}{4} \\ \hline \end{array}$

14. $\begin{array}{r} 9\frac{3}{5} \\ + 6\frac{1}{5} \\ \hline \end{array}$

15. $5\frac{1}{4} + 12\frac{1}{4}$ _____

Solve. Write your answer in simplest form.

16. Phoebe buys $1\frac{1}{8}$ pounds of cashew nuts and $1\frac{3}{8}$ pounds of peanuts.

    How many pounds of nuts does she buy in all? _____

Adding Mixed Numbers (B)

Practice Adding Mixed Numbers with Regrouping

Find the sum. Write your answer in simplest form.

1. $5\frac{2}{5} + 6\frac{4}{5}$

   a. Add the whole number parts of the mixed numbers.

   $5 + 6 =$ _____

   b. Add the fraction parts of the mixed numbers and simplify the improper fraction.

   $\frac{2}{5} + \frac{4}{5} =$ _____

   c. What is the sum in simplest form?

   $5\frac{2}{5} + 6\frac{4}{5} =$ _____

2. $4\frac{3}{5} + 8\frac{3}{5}$ _____

3. $3\frac{7}{12} + 2\frac{5}{12}$ _____

4. $\begin{aligned} &1\frac{95}{100} \\ +\ &2\frac{15}{100} \end{aligned}$

5. $\begin{aligned} &3\frac{4}{6} \\ +\ &7\frac{5}{6} \end{aligned}$

6. $19\frac{7}{8} + 5\frac{6}{8}$ _____

7. $5\frac{3}{10} + 3\frac{7}{10}$ _____

8. $8\frac{2}{4}$
   $+5\frac{3}{4}$
   $\overline{\phantom{+5\frac{3}{4}}}$

9. $2\frac{11}{12}$
   $+5\frac{5}{12}$
   $\overline{\phantom{+5\frac{5}{12}}}$

10. $1\frac{4}{5} + 4\frac{3}{5}$ _____

11. $9\frac{6}{8} + 5\frac{4}{8}$ _____

12. $4\frac{7}{12}$
    $+6\frac{9}{12}$
    $\overline{\phantom{+6\frac{9}{12}}}$

13. $30\frac{4}{8}$
    $+12\frac{7}{8}$
    $\overline{\phantom{+12\frac{7}{8}}}$

14. $2\frac{3}{6} + 6\frac{4}{6}$ _____

15. $11\frac{7}{10} + 9\frac{7}{10}$ _____

Solve. Write your answer in simplest form.

16. Jake walks $2\frac{3}{4}$ miles to the store and $2\frac{3}{4}$ miles back.

    How many miles did Jake walk altogether? _____

Subtracting Mixed Numbers (A)

Practice Subtracting Mixed Numbers Without Regrouping

Find the difference. Write your answer in simplest form.

1. $8\frac{9}{12} - 4\frac{7}{12}$

   a. Subtract the whole number parts of the mixed numbers.

   $8 - 4 =$ _____

   b. Subtract the fraction parts of the mixed numbers and simplify.

   $\frac{9}{12} - \frac{7}{12} =$ _____

   c. What is the difference in simplest form?

   $8\frac{9}{12} - 4\frac{7}{12} =$ _____

2. $15\frac{4}{5} - 12\frac{3}{5}$ _____

3. $3\frac{15}{100} - 2\frac{5}{100}$ _____

4. $9\frac{5}{8}$
   $-2\frac{2}{8}$
   _____

5. $11\frac{4}{6}$
   $-1\frac{4}{6}$
   _____

6. $7\frac{3}{4} - 2\frac{2}{4}$ _____

7. $5\frac{5}{6} - 5\frac{3}{6}$ _____

8. $\begin{array}{r} 8\frac{9}{10} \\ -\ 6\frac{7}{10} \\ \hline \end{array}$

9. $\begin{array}{r} 19\frac{7}{8} \\ -3\frac{2}{8} \\ \hline \end{array}$

10. $13\frac{8}{10} - 3\frac{1}{10}$ _____

11. $20\frac{2}{3} - 1\frac{1}{3}$ _____

12. $\begin{array}{r} 14\frac{9}{100} \\ -\ 11\frac{6}{100} \\ \hline \end{array}$

13. $\begin{array}{r} 5\frac{7}{12} \\ -\ 3\frac{1}{12} \\ \hline \end{array}$

14. $\begin{array}{r} 10\frac{3}{5} \\ -\ 5\frac{1}{5} \\ \hline \end{array}$

15. $6\frac{5}{8} - 2\frac{3}{8}$ _____

Solve. Write your answer in simplest form.

16. Juan has $2\frac{3}{4}$ cups of flour. He uses $1\frac{1}{4}$ cups of the flour to bake cookies.

    How many cups of flour does Juan have left? _____

Subtracting Mixed Numbers (B)

Practice Subtracting Mixed Numbers with Regrouping

Find the difference. Write your answer in simplest form.

1. $11\frac{1}{5} - 6\frac{3}{5}$

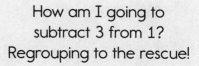

How am I going to subtract 3 from 1? Regrouping to the rescue!

    a. Regroup $11\frac{1}{5}$.

        $11\frac{1}{5} =$ _____

    b. Subtract the fraction parts of the mixed numbers.

        $\frac{6}{5} - \frac{3}{5} =$ _____

    c. Subtract the whole number parts.

        $10 - 6 =$ _____

    d. What is the difference in simplest form?

        $11\frac{1}{5} - 6\frac{3}{5} =$ _____

2. $3\frac{1}{3} - 1\frac{2}{3}$ _____

3. $9\frac{3}{12} - 3\frac{5}{12}$ _____

4. $10\frac{3}{10}$
$-\ 8\frac{5}{10}$
_____

5. $6\frac{2}{6}$
$-\ 2\frac{5}{6}$
_____

6. $15\frac{1}{8} - 5\frac{3}{8}$ _____

7. $8\frac{1}{4} - 3\frac{2}{4}$ _____

8. $7\frac{7}{12}$
   $-5\frac{11}{12}$
   _____

9. $16\frac{2}{8}$
   $-11\frac{5}{8}$
   _____

10. $4\frac{2}{5} - 2\frac{3}{5}$ _____

11. $8\frac{5}{10} - 4\frac{9}{10}$ _____

12. $12\frac{5}{12}$
    $-5\frac{10}{12}$
    _____

13. $9\frac{4}{8}$
    $-4\frac{7}{8}$
    _____

14. $7\frac{3}{6} - \frac{5}{6}$ _____

15. $14\frac{2}{10} - 10\frac{7}{10}$ _____

Solve. Write your answer in simplest form.

16. Simon has $3\frac{1}{4}$ pounds of cheese. He uses $\frac{3}{4}$ pound for sandwiches.

    How many pounds of cheese does Simon have left? _____

Problem Solving with Mixed Numbers (A)

Practice Adding Fractions and Mixed Numbers to Solve Problems

Solve. Write your answer in simplest form. Convert improper fractions to mixed numbers.

1. Sally is making dessert. The recipe uses $\frac{2}{3}$ cup of blueberries and $\frac{2}{3}$ cup of strawberries.

   How many cups of berries does Sally need in all?

   a. What do you need to find to solve the problem?

   _____

   _____

   b. What information does the problem give you?

   _____

   _____

   _____

   c. Is there a word or phrase in the problem that could be a clue for the operation you need to use? If so, what is the word or phrase?

   _____

   _____

   d. What operation do you use to solve the problem? _____

   e. How many cups of berries does Sally need? _____

2. Serena swims $\frac{1}{4}$ mile on Saturday. She swims $\frac{2}{4}$ mile on Sunday.

   How many miles does Serena swim altogether? _____

3. Alex has $\frac{5}{8}$ pound of nuts. He buys $\frac{7}{8}$ pound more of nuts.

   How many pounds of nuts does Alex have in all? _____

4. The table shows the weights of different dog breeds.

   What is the total weight of the beagle and poodle combined? _____

Breed	Weight (lb)
beagle	$20\frac{3}{8}$
fox terrier	$16\frac{6}{8}$
poodle	$11\frac{4}{8}$
pug	$14\frac{1}{8}$

AKC Staff 2017

5. Michael watches two movies. The first movie is $1\frac{2}{3}$ hours long.
   The second movie is $2\frac{2}{3}$ hours long.

   How many hours in all does Michael spend watching movies? _____

6. Simon drinks $1\frac{1}{2}$ cups of milk twice a day.

   How many cups of milk does Simon drink each day? _____

Practice Subtracting Fractions and Mixed Numbers

Solve. Write your answer in simplest form.

1. A 25-gallon fish tank is $24\frac{2}{8}$ inches long. A 50-gallon fish tank is $36\frac{7}{8}$ inches long.

   How much longer is the 50-gallon tank than the 25-gallon tank?

   a. What do you need to find to solve the problem?

   b. What information does the problem give you?

   c. Is there a word or phrase in the problem that could be a clue for the operation you need to use? If so, what is the word or phrase?

   d. What operation do you use to solve the problem? _____

   e. How much longer is the 50-gallon tank than the 25-gallon tank? _____

2. Dion practices the piano for $\frac{10}{12}$ hour on Monday. He practices for $\frac{6}{12}$ hour on Tuesday.

   How much more does Dion practice on Monday than on Tuesday? _____

3. Marcus hikes a trail that is $7\frac{4}{10}$ kilometers long. Kayla hikes a different trail that is $5\frac{7}{10}$ kilometers long.

   How much longer is the trail that Marcus hikes? _____

4. The table shows the mass of different insects.

   How much more does a grasshopper weigh than a bee? _____

Insect	Mass (g)
bee	$\frac{1}{10}$
cricket	$\frac{3}{10}$
grasshopper	$\frac{5}{10}$
wasp	$\frac{2}{10}$

5. At the beginning of the year, Mae was $48\frac{7}{8}$ inches tall. At the end of the year, she is $51\frac{1}{8}$ inches tall.

   How many inches does Mae grow during the year? _____

6. Laurie has $5\frac{1}{3}$ cups of orange juice. After she drinks some orange juice, she has $3\frac{2}{3}$ cups of juice left.

   How many cups of juice does Laurie drink? _____

Problem Solving with Mixed Numbers (C)

Practice Solving Problems with Fractions and Mixed Numbers

Solve. Write your answer in simplest form.

1. Jenna is making trail mix. She has $\frac{4}{8}$ cup of raisins in her cupboard and and buys $\frac{5}{8}$ cup more raisins. Jenna uses $\frac{6}{8}$ cup of raisins in the trail mix.

   How many cups of raisins are left?

   a. What do you need to find to solve the problem?

   _____

   _____

   b. What information does the problem give you?

   _____

   _____

   c. Describe how you will solve the problem.

   _____

   _____

   _____

   d. What operations do you use to solve the problem?

   _____

   e. How many cups of raisins are left? _____

2. Carla bakes 2 pans of lasagna. Her family eats $1\frac{1}{3}$ pans. Carla gives her neighbor $\frac{1}{3}$ pan.

How much lasagna is left? _____

3. Sela buys 2 packages of turkey. Each package weighs $\frac{7}{8}$ pound. Sela uses $\frac{2}{8}$ pound of the turkey for a sandwich.

   a. Describe two ways to find how many pounds of turkey are left.

   _____

   _____

   _____

   _____

   b. How many pounds of turkey are left? _____

4. The table shows the distances Freddie walks each day. What is the total

   number of kilometers he walks on Monday, Tuesday, and Wednesday? _____

Day	Distance (km)
Monday	$1\frac{3}{10}$
Tuesday	$2\frac{1}{10}$
Wednesday	$1\frac{2}{10}$
Thursday	$2\frac{4}{10}$

5. Dara has $2\frac{6}{12}$ jars of red beads and $2\frac{3}{12}$ jars of blue beads. She mixes

   the beads together and then uses $\frac{7}{12}$ jar of them to make necklaces.

   How many jars of beads are left? _____

Multiplication with Arrays (A)

Practice Multiplying with Arrays and Area Models

Write the multiplication expression that the array models.

1.

Use the array to find the product.

2.

$16 \times 7 =$ _____

Complete the area model to find the product.

3. 46×8

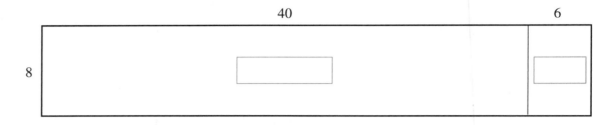

$46 \times 8 =$ _____ $+ 48 =$ _____

4. 54×7

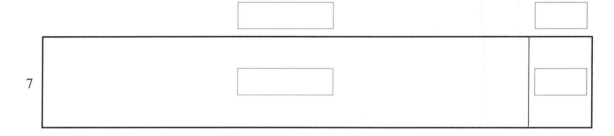

$54 \times 7 =$ _____ $+$ _____ $=$ _____

5. 63×5

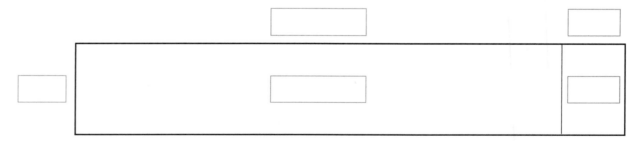

$63 \times 5 =$ _____ $+$ _____ $=$ _____

Multiplication with Arrays (B)

Practice Multiplying 3 Digits by 1 Digit with Area Models

Multiply.

> Using a model helps me understand multiplication.

1. $6 \times 100 =$ _____

2. $14 \times 100 =$ _____

3. $3 \times 200 =$ _____

4. $6 \times 700 =$ _____

Complete the area model to find the product.

5. 4×397

	300	90	7
4	[ ]	[ ]	[ ]

$4 \times 397 =$ _____ $+$ _____ $+ 28 =$ _____

6. 852×7

	800	50	2
7	[ ]	[ ]	[ ]

$852 \times 7 =$ _____ $+$ _____ $+$ _____ $=$ _____

7. 6×485

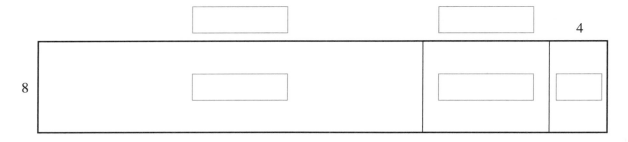

$6 \times 485 = $ _____

8. 674×8

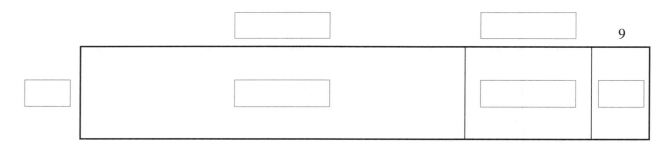

$674 \times 8 = $ _____

9. 839×6

$839 \times 6 = $ _____

Practice Multiplying 2 Digits by 1 Digit Using Equations

Multiply using equations.

1. $23 \times 6 = ($ _____ $+$ _____ $) \times$ _____

   $=$ _____ $\times 6 + 3 \times$ _____

   $=$ _____ $+$ _____

   $=$ _____

2. $3 \times 87 =$ _____ $\times ($ _____ $+$ _____ $)$

   $=$ _____ $\times 80 + 3 \times$ _____

   $=$ _____ $+$ _____

   $=$ _____

3. $49 \times 8 = ($ _____ $+$ _____ $) \times$ _____

   $=$ _____ $\times$ _____ $+$ _____ $\times$ _____

   $=$ _____ $+$ _____

   $=$ _____

4. $5 \times 93 =$ _____ $\times ($ _____ $+$ _____ $)$

   $=$ _____ $\times$ _____ $+$ _____ $\times$ _____

   $=$ _____ $+$ _____

   $=$ _____

Multiply using equations. Show all your work.

5. 89×5

6. 74×6

7. 3×52

8. 83×5

9. 9×76

10. 7×29

11. 4×39

12. 67×8

Practice Multiplying 3 Digits by 1 Digit Using Equations

Multiply using equations.

1. $375 \times 6 = ($ _____ $+$ _____ $+ 5) \times 6$

   $=$ _____ $\times 6 + 70 \times$ _____ $+ 5 \times 6$

   $=$ _____ $+$ _____ $+$ _____

   $=$ _____

2. $7 \times 284 = 7 \times ($ _____ $+$ _____ $+$ _____ $)$

   $=$ _____ $\times 200 + 7 \times$ _____ $+ 7 \times$ _____

   $=$ _____ $+$ _____ $+$ _____

   $=$ _____

3. $428 \times 9 = ($ _____ $+$ _____ $+$ _____ $) \times$ _____

   $=$ _____ $\times$ _____ $+$ _____ $\times$ _____ $+$ _____ $\times$ _____

   $=$ _____ $+$ _____ $+$ _____

   $=$ _____

4. $3 \times 643 =$ _____ $\times ($ _____ $+$ _____ $+$ _____ $)$

   $=$ _____ $\times$ _____ $+$ _____ $\times$ _____ $+$ _____ $\times$ _____

   $=$ _____ $+$ _____ $+$ _____

   $=$ _____

Multiply using equations. Show all your work.

5. 193×8

6. 736×6

7. 4×578

8. 861×5

9. 2×503

10. 9×240

11. 4×733

12. 279×3

Multiplication Using Algorithm (A)

Practice Multiplying 2 Digits by 1 Digit Using Algorithm

Estimate the product.

1. 78×4 _____

2. 63×7 _____

3. 57×8 _____

Multiply using the standard algorithm.

4.
```
      4  1
  ×      7
  ☐  ☐  ☐
```

5.
```
      5  3
  ×      3
  ☐  ☐  ☐
```

6.
```
      9  2
  ×      4
  ☐  ☐  ☐
```

7.
```
      3  8
  ×      5
  ☐  ☐  0
```

8.
```
      7  3
  ×      9
  ☐  ☐  ☐
```

9.
```
      4  8
  ×      7
  ☐  ☐  ☐
```

10.
```
      1  4
  ×      8
  ☐  ☐  ☐
```

11.
```
      3  4
  ×      7
  ☐  ☐  ☐
```

12.
```
      7  6
  ×      4
  ☐  ☐  ☐
```

13.
$$\begin{array}{r} 1\ 9 \\ \times\quad\ 5 \\ \hline \end{array}$$
☐☐☐

14.
$$\begin{array}{r} 5\ 6 \\ \times\quad\ 9 \\ \hline \end{array}$$
☐☐☐

15.
$$\begin{array}{r} 8\ 2 \\ \times\quad\ 3 \\ \hline \end{array}$$
☐☐☐

Multiply. Then, use estimation to explain why the solution makes sense.

16.
$$\begin{array}{r} 3\ 6 \\ \times\quad\ 5 \\ \hline \end{array}$$
☐☐☐

17.
$$\begin{array}{r} 6\ 8 \\ \times\quad\ 3 \\ \hline \end{array}$$
☐☐☐

18.
$$\begin{array}{r} 5\ 4 \\ \times\quad\ 6 \\ \hline \end{array}$$
☐☐☐

19.
$$\begin{array}{r} 8\ 2 \\ \times\quad\ 5 \\ \hline \end{array}$$
☐☐☐

Multiplication Using Algorithm (B)

Practice Multiplying 3 Digits by 1 Digit Using Algorithm

Use benchmarks to estimate the product.

1. 723×8 _____

2. 582×4 _____

3. 453×6 _____

4. 341×7 _____

Multiply using the standard algorithm.

5.
$$\begin{array}{r} 6\ \ 2\ \ 1 \\ \times\ \ \ \ \ \ \ 4 \\ \hline \square\ \square\ \square\ \square \end{array}$$

6.
$$\begin{array}{r} 1\ \ 3\ \ 4 \\ \times\ \ \ \ \ \ \ 2 \\ \hline \square\ \square\ \square \end{array}$$

7.
$$\begin{array}{r} 5\ \ 2\ \ 3 \\ \times\ \ \ \ \ \ \ 4 \\ \hline \square\ \square\ \square\ \square \end{array}$$

8.
$$\begin{array}{r} 7\ \ 2\ \ 5 \\ \times\ \ \ \ \ \ \ 3 \\ \hline \square\ \square\ \square\ \square \end{array}$$

9.
$$\begin{array}{r} 7\ \ 8\ \ 1 \\ \times\ \ \ \ \ \ \ 5 \\ \hline \square\ \square\ \square\ \square \end{array}$$

10.
$$\begin{array}{r} 6\ \ 4\ \ 8 \\ \times\ \ \ \ \ \ \ 9 \\ \hline \square\ \square\ \square\ \square \end{array}$$

11.
$$
\begin{array}{r}
2\ 6\ 3 \\
\times\qquad 3 \\
\hline
\square\ \square\ \square
\end{array}
$$

12.
$$
\begin{array}{r}
3\ 8\ 1 \\
\times\qquad 7 \\
\hline
\square\ \square\ \square\ \square
\end{array}
$$

13.
$$
\begin{array}{r}
4\ 7\ 5 \\
\times\qquad 8 \\
\hline
\square\ \square\ \square\ \square
\end{array}
$$

14.
$$
\begin{array}{r}
3\ 6\ 4 \\
\times\qquad 3 \\
\hline
\square\ \square\ \square\ \square
\end{array}
$$

15.
$$
\begin{array}{r}
1\ 3\ 9 \\
\times\qquad 6 \\
\hline
\square\ \square\ \square
\end{array}
$$

16.
$$
\begin{array}{r}
4\ 3\ 8 \\
\times\qquad 2 \\
\hline
\square\ \square\ \square
\end{array}
$$

Multiply. Then, use estimation to explain why the product makes sense.

17.
$$
\begin{array}{r}
9\ 2\ 2 \\
\times\qquad 4 \\
\hline
\square\ \square\ \square\ \square
\end{array}
$$

_____

_____

18.
$$
\begin{array}{r}
8\ 5\ 7 \\
\times\qquad 3 \\
\hline
\square\ \square\ \square\ \square
\end{array}
$$

_____

_____

19.
$$
\begin{array}{r}
7\ 8\ 5 \\
\times\qquad 9 \\
\hline
\square\ \square\ \square\ \square
\end{array}
$$

_____

_____

Problem Solving with Multidigit Multiplication (A)

Practice Comparing and Evaluating with Multiplication

Solve.

1. Jordan plays basketball for 45 minutes on Monday. He plays 3 times as long on Saturday as he did on Monday.

   How many minutes does Jordan play basketball on Saturday? _____

2. Kiki reads 26 pages of her book on Tuesday. She reads 4 times as many pages on Thursday as she did on Tuesday.

   How many pages does Kiki read on Thursday? _____

3. Juan has 38 baseball cards in his collection. Evan has 6 times as many cards as Juan in his collection.

   How many baseball cards does Evan have in his collection? _____

4. Sarah compares the number of calories in two different meals. Meal A has 564 calories. Meal B has 3 times as many calories as Meal A.

   How many calories are in Meal B? _____

5. Pleasantville is 198 miles from Happytown. Giggleton is 8 times as far from Happytown as Pleasantville.

   How many miles from Happytown is Giggleton? _____

6. Raj sees a black bear and a giraffe at the zoo. The bear weighs 238 pounds. The giraffe weighs 8 times as much as the bear.

   How much does the giraffe weigh? _____

Evaluate.

7. $78 \times 6 + 126 - 3 \times 148$ _____

8. $156 + 249 \times 3 - 6 \times 78$ _____

9. $899 - 219 \times 4 + 28$ _____

10. $798 + 34 - 6 \times 87$ _____

11. $56 + 39 \times 4 \times 3$ _____

12. $43 \times 6 - 4 \times 38$ _____

Don't forget to always multiply from left to right first.

13. $187 \times 4 - 15 \times 3 + 78$ _____

14. $328 \times 3 - 4 \times 229$ _____

Problem Solving with Multidigit Multiplication (B)

Practice Solving Problems with 2-Digit Multiplication

Solve.

1. Eloise babysits for 3 weeks and does chores for 4 weeks. She earns $96 each week babysitting and $24 each week doing chores.

    a. Let d represent the total amount of money Eloise earns. Write an equation that models how much Eloise earns.

    _____

    b. Solve for d. _____

    c. How much money does Eloise earn in all? _____

2. Raj and Matthew play a video game. Raj scores 96 points. Matthew scores 3 times as many points as Raj.

    How many more points does Matthew score than Raj? _____

3. Jada has $32 in her piggy bank. On Monday, she earns another $46. On Tuesday, she earns 2 times as much as Monday. On Wednesday, she spends $27.

    How much money does Jada have left after she spends $27? _____

4. Juan plans to buy 5 shirts for $24 each, 3 pairs of pants for $36 each, and 2 pairs of shoes for $38 each.

    How much money will Juan spend on all these items? _____

5. Min reads 19 pages of his book on Friday. He reads 4 times as many pages on Sunday as he did on Friday.

   How many more pages does Min read on Sunday than on Friday? _____

6. James is raising money for charity. He collects $78 in week 1. He collects 3 times as much money in week 2 as he did in week 1. He collects $92 in week 3. He concludes that he has raised a total of $326.

   Is James's answer reasonable? Explain.

   _____

   _____

   _____

7. Maria does 18 sit-ups. Natalie does 5 times as many sit-ups as Maria. Natalie concludes that she has done 72 more sit-ups than Maria.

   Is Natalie's answer reasonable? Explain.

   _____

   _____

   _____

8. Sarah is going shopping. She plans to purchase 6 items. One item costs $17, 2 items cost $21, and 3 items cost $23. She concludes that she will have to pay $228.

   Is Sarah's answer reasonable? Explain.

   _____

   _____

   _____

   _____

Problem Solving with Multidigit Multiplication (C)

Practice Solving Problems with 3-Digit Multiplication

Solve.

1. On Wednesday, 538 people attend a play. Three times as many people attend the play on Saturday as did on Wednesday. Let n represent how many more people attend the play on Saturday than on Wednesday.

   a. Write an equation that models how many more people attend the play on Saturday than on Wednesday.

   _____

   b. How many more people attend the play on Saturday than

   on Wednesday? _____

2. Juan and his family travel 386 miles per day on Monday and Tuesday. Then, they travel 482 miles per day on Wednesday, Thursday, and Friday.

   How many miles does Juan's family travel in all? _____

3. Ethan and some friends order 3 slices of pizza and 2 grilled chicken sandwiches for lunch. Each slice of pizza contains 285 calories. Each grilled chicken sandwich contains 419 calories.

   What is the total number of calories in all the lunch items combined? _____

4. Seven storage containers are loaded on to a truck. Two containers weigh 114 pounds each, 3 containers weigh 185 pounds each, and 2 containers weigh 204 pounds each.

   How many pounds are loaded on to the truck in all? _____

5. Danville is 482 miles from Roxbury. Victorsburg is 7 times as far from Roxbury as Danville. Evan determines that Victorsburg is 2,374 more miles from Roxbury than Danville is from Roxbury.

   Is Evan's answer reasonable? Explain.

   _____

   _____

   _____

6. Kiki's parents purchase 2 armchairs for $287 each and 2 end tables for $124 each. Kiki concludes that her parents pay a total of $1,644.

   Is Kiki's answer reasonable? Explain.

   _____

   _____

   _____

7. Raj, Eloise, and Aisha play a video game as a team. Raj scores 304 points, Eloise scores 112 points, and Aisha scores 4 times as many points as Eloise. Raj determines that they score 864 points altogether.

   Is Raj's answer reasonable? Explain.

   _____

   _____

   _____

   _____

Multiples of 10 (A)

Practice Multiplying Multiples of 10 Using Models

Solve.

1. Use the area model to multiply 10 × 90.

	10	10	10	10	10	10	10	10	10
10	100	100	100	100	100	100	100	100	100

   a. What is the side length of each of the 9 squares that make up the model?

     _____ units

   b. What is the area of each square in the model? _____ square units

   c. Describe how to use the model to find the product.

     _____

     _____

   d. What is the product? _____

2. Use the area model to find 40 × 50. _____

	10	10	10	10	10
10	100	100	100	100	100
10	100	100	100	100	100
10	100	100	100	100	100
10	100	100	100	100	100

3. Draw an area model to find 10×30. _____

4. Draw an area model to find 50×30. _____

Answer the question.

5. What do you notice about the number of zeros in the factors and the number of zeros in the product when you multiply two numbers that are multiples of 10?

   _____

   _____

   _____

Multiples of 10 (B)

Practice Multiplying a Multiple of 10 by a Number Using Models

Solve.

1. Use the area model to multiply 10 × 47.

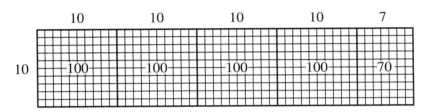

a. What figures make up this area model?

_____ squares and _____ rectangle

b. What are the dimensions of each figure in the model?

_____

_____

c. What is the area of each figure in the model?

_____

_____

_____

d. Describe how to use the model to find the product.

_____

_____

e. What is the product? _____

2. Use the area model to find 20×39. _____

	10	10	10	9
10	100	100	100	90
10	100	100	100	90

3. Draw an area model to find 38×50. _____

4. Draw an area model to find 63×10. _____

Answer the question.

5. Azra draws this area model to find 25×10. What mistake does Azra make? Correct her error and find the product.

	20	5
10	100	50

_____

_____

Multiples of 10 (C)

Practice Multiplying with Multiples of 10 Using Shortcut

Solve.

1. Use a shortcut to multiply 20×15.

   a. Multiply 15 by the tens digit in the multiple of 10.

      What is this product? _____

   b. Add a zero to the product from Part (a) to find 20×15.

      What is 20×15? _____

Find the product.

2. 80×10 _____

3. 21×30 _____

4. 15×10 _____

5. 60×18 _____

6. 10×99 _____

7. 80×21 _____

8. 70×68 _____

9. 19×30 _____

Answer the question.

10. Candace multiplies 40×70 and says the product is 280. Is Candace correct? If she is **not** correct, explain her error and solve the problem.

_____

_____

_____

11. Lila has 10 pieces of ribbon. Each piece of ribbon is 22 inches long.

    How many inches of ribbon does Lila have in all? _____

12. James earns $20 for each lawn he mows.
    This week, James mows 18 lawns.

    How much money does James earn this week? _____

13. Explain how the product $31 \times 5 = 155$ can help you find the product 31×50.

_____

_____

I love using shortcuts in math!

Multiplying Two 2-Digit Numbers (A)

Practice Multiplying 2-Digit Numbers Using Area Models

Solve.

1. Use the area model to multiply 54 × 36.

	50	4
30		
6		

a. How many parts make up this area model? _____

b. What are the dimensions of each of the parts of the model?

_____

_____

_____

c. Label each part of the model with its area.

d. Describe how to use the model to find the product.

_____

_____

_____

e. What is the product? _____

2. Draw an area model to find 41×65. _____

3. Draw an area model to find 29×26. _____

Answer the questions.

4. What multiplication problem is shown in the model?
What is the product?

_____

Multiplying Two 2-Digit Numbers (B)

Practice Estimating to Multiply 2-Digit Numbers

Solve.

1. Use rounding to estimate the product 28 × 72.

   a. Round the first factor, 28. _____

   b. Round the second factor, 72. _____

   c. Multiply the two rounded factors to estimate. _____

Estimate the product using rounding.

2. 12 × 18 _____

3. 68 × 27 _____

4. 48 × 48 _____

5. 21 × 59 _____

6. 73 × 89 _____

7. 11 × 52 _____

8. 74 × 54 _____

9. 42 × 36 _____

> Rounding to the nearest 10 is a great skill to master.

Estimate the product using compatible numbers.

10. 28×31 _____

11. 11×59 _____

12. 23×68 _____

13. 14×19 _____

Answer the question.

14. Rani saves $22 each month. About how much does Rani save in 12 months?

_____

_____

_____

15. Michael states that 39×81 is 351. Use estimation to determine whether Michael's answer is reasonable. Is Michael's answer reasonable? Explain.

_____

_____

_____

_____

Multiplying Two 2-Digit Numbers (C)

Practice Multiplying 2-Digit Numbers Using Algorithm

Solve.

1. Multiply.

$$\begin{array}{r} 64 \\ \times\, 43 \\ \hline \end{array}$$

    a. Multiply 64 × 3 to find the first partial product. _____

    b. What do you multiply to find the second partial product? _____

    c. What is the second partial product? _____

    d. What is the product? _____

Fill in the missing numbers to multiply.

2.
$$\begin{array}{r} 2\;4 \\ \times\; 1\;5 \\ \hline 1\;\square\;0 \\ +\;\square\;\;4\;0 \\ \hline \square\;\square\;0 \end{array}$$

3.
$$\begin{array}{r} 5\;\;7 \\ \times\;\; 3\;\;6 \\ \hline 3\;4\;\square \\ +\;1,\square\;\square\;0 \\ \hline 2,\square\;\square\;\square \end{array}$$

Multiply.

4. 23×52 _____

5. 22×22 _____

6. 72×84 _____

7. 11×81 _____

8.
$$\begin{array}{r} 15 \\ \times\ 45 \\ \hline \end{array}$$

9.
$$\begin{array}{r} 86 \\ \times\ 38 \\ \hline \end{array}$$

10.
$$\begin{array}{r} 72 \\ \times\ 33 \\ \hline \end{array}$$

11.
$$\begin{array}{r} 91 \\ \times\ 81 \\ \hline \end{array}$$

Answer the question.

12. Sammi multiplies 41×51. Her work is shown. Does she multiply correctly? Explain.

$$\begin{array}{r} 41 \\ \times\ 51 \\ \hline 41 \\ +\ 205 \\ \hline 246 \end{array}$$

_____

_____

Problem Solving with 2-Digit Multiplication (A)

Practice Multiplying Multiples of 10 in Real-World Problems

Solve.

1. Jackson orders pizzas from Dave's Pizzeria for a family reunion. He orders 16 cheese pizzas, 12 veggie pizzas, and 10 pepperoni pizzas. Jackson has $500 to spend on pizza.

Dave's Pizzeria	
Pizza type	Cost
cheese	$10
veggie	$12
pepperoni	$15

a. How much do the cheese pizzas cost? _____

b. How much do the veggie pizzas cost? _____

c. How much do the pepperoni pizzas cost? _____

d. What is the total cost for the pizzas? _____

e. How much money does Jackson have left after he pays for the pizzas? _____

2. A gardener plants 25 tomato plants. She estimates that each plant will produce 30 pounds of tomatoes. She plans on selling them at the farmers market for $4 per pound.

   How much money can she expect to make? _____

3. There are 18 rows of seats in a theater. Each row has 20 seats in it. There are 225 people in the theater.

   How many empty seats are there? _____

4. Mr. Gonzales drives 18 miles each way to work each day.

   a. Write an equation that can be used to find the number of miles Mr. Gonzales drives to and from work in 30 days.
      Use *m* for the unknown.

      _____

   b. How many miles does Mr. Gonzales drive to and from work in 30 days? _____

5. There are 60 people on a cruise boat that sails around a harbor. Forty people are adults and the rest are children. An adult ticket costs $18 and a child ticket costs $12.

   Use rounding to estimate how much the tickets cost in all for the 60 people.

   _____

6. Joe charges $20 for each lawn he mows. He mows 18 lawns this week. He uses $125 of the money he earns to buy an activity tracker.

   a. Write an equation that can be used to find how much money Joe has left after he buys the tracker. Use *m* for the unknown.

      _____

   b. How much money does Joe have left after he buys the tracker? _____

Problem Solving with 2-Digit Multiplication (B)

Practice Multiplying 2-Digit Numbers in Real-World Problems

Solve.

1. The members of a tour group are taking a boat ride. There are 21 adults, 15 children, and 12 senior citizens in the group.

Boat Rides	
Ticket type	Price
adult	$22
child	$18
senior citizen	$16

a. How much does it cost for the adults to ride the boat? _____

b. How much does it cost for the children to ride the boat? _____

c. How much does it cost for the senior citizens to ride the boat? _____

d. What is the total cost for all the members of the tour group to

ride the boat? _____

2. Kiki buys a 2 boxes of trading cards. Each box contains 24 packs of cards. Each pack has 12 cards.

How many cards does Kiki buy in all? _____

3. Diana is catering a party. She bakes 14 pans of lasagna. Each pan uses 12 ounces of cheese. Diana buys 15 bags of shredded cheese. Each bag contains 16 ounces of cheese.

a. Write an equation that can be used to find how many ounces of cheese Diana has left over. Use a for the unknown.

_____

b. How many ounces of cheese are left over? _____

4. Selma has $225 in her savings account. She saves $25 each month for the next 24 months.

How much does Selma have in her savings account after 24 months? _____

5. Peter solves this problem.

A chef has 14 cartons of eggs. He buys 21 more cartons of eggs. Each carton contains 18 eggs. How many eggs does the chef have now?

Peter says the chef has 630 eggs.

Use estimation to determine whether Peter's answer is reasonable. Justify your answer.

_____

_____

_____

_____

Division with Models (A)

Practice Using Models to Divide 2 Digits by 1 Digit

Use the array to divide.

1. $70 \div 5 =$ _____

2. $96 \div 6 =$ _____

Use the area model to divide.

3. $72 \div 3 =$ _____

```
                                        20                    ┌──────────┐
                                                              │          │
                                                              └──────────┘
        ┌──────────────────────────────────────────┬──────────────────┐
     3  │                    60                     │    ┌──────────┐   │
        │                                           │    │          │   │
        │                                           │    └──────────┘   │
        └──────────────────────────────────────────┴──────────────────┘
```

4. $96 \div 2 =$ _____

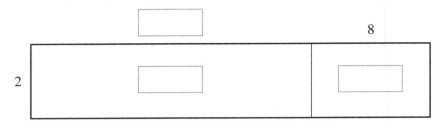

5. $95 \div 5 =$ _____

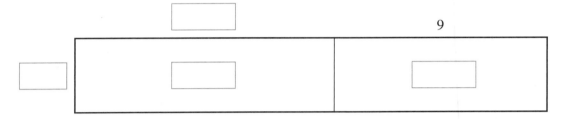

Create an area model to divide. Then, complete the equations that describe the division calculation.

6. $92 \div 4$

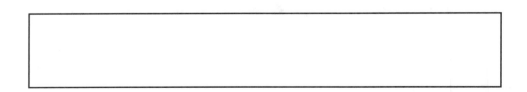

$92 \div 4 =$ _____ $\div$ _____ $+$ _____ $\div$ _____

$=$ _____ $+$ _____

$=$ _____

Division with Models (B)

Practice Using Models to Divide 3 Digits by 1 Digit

Complete the area model to divide.

1. $712 \div 4 =$ _____

	[ ]		[ ]	8
4	400		[ ]	32

2. $819 \div 3 =$ _____

	[ ]		[ ]	[ ]
3	[ ]		[ ]	9

3. $564 \div 6 =$ _____

	[ ]		[ ]
6	[ ]		24

4. $912 \div 3 =$ _____

	☐	☐
3	☐	12

Create an area model to divide. Then, complete the equations that describe the division calculation.

5. $815 \div 5$

$815 \div 5 =$ _____ $\div$ _____ $+$ _____ $\div$ _____ $+$

_____ $\div$ _____

$=$ _____ $+$ _____ $+$ _____

$=$ _____

Who knew models could be so helpful?

Division Algorithm Without Remainders (A)

Practice Using the Algorithm to Divide 2 or 3 Digits by 1 Digit

Divide the two-digit number by the one-digit number.

1.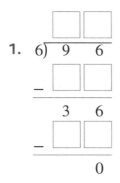
$$6\overline{)\ 9\ \ 6}$$

2. $4\overline{)\ 7\ \ 2}$

3. $3\overline{)\ 9\ \ 3}$

4. $7\overline{)\ 9\ \ 8}$

5. $87 \div 3 =$ _____

6. $78 \div 6 =$ _____

Divide the three-digit number by the one-digit number.

7.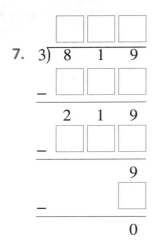

$$3\overline{)819}$$

8.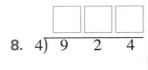

$$4\overline{)924}$$

9. $658 \div 7 =$ _____

10. $920 \div 4 =$ _____

11. $8\overline{)872}$

12. $7\overline{)623}$

Division Algorithm Without Remainders (B)

Practice Dividing by 1 Digit in Comparison Problems

Estimate the quotient using rounding and benchmark numbers to determine whether Aisha's solution is reasonable.

1. Aisha determines that $228 \div 6 = 38$.

    a. Round 228 to the nearest hundred. _____

    b. Is 6 between benchmark numbers 1 and 5 or 5 and 10?

    _____

    c. Divide your answer in Part (a) by the two benchmark numbers 6 is

    between. _____

    d. Refer to your answer in Part (b). Which benchmark number is

    6 closer to? _____

    e. Complete the sentence.

    The quotient $228 \div 6$ is between _____ and _____,

    but it is closer to _____. Therefore, Aisha's solution is reasonable.

Estimate using compatible numbers.

2. $336 \div 8 \approx$ _____ $\div$ _____ $\approx$ _____

3. $438 \div 6 \approx$ _____ $\div$ _____ $\approx$ _____

4. $656 \div 8 \approx$ _____ $\div$ _____ $\approx$ _____

5. $468 \div 9 \approx$ _____ $\div$ _____ $\approx$ _____

6. $231 \div 7 \approx$ _____ $\div$ _____ $\approx$ _____

Solve.

7. Raj reads 144 pages of his book. That is 6 times the number of pages that Min reads of his book.

   How many pages does Min read? _____

8. Rami weighs two containers. The first container weighs 104 pounds. That is 4 times the number of pounds that the second container weighs.

   How many pounds does the second container weigh? _____

9. Natalie travels 294 miles in one day. That is 7 times the number of miles Jordan travels that day.

   How many miles does Jordan travel? _____

10. Town A is 744 miles from Town B. That is 4 times the distance than Town C is from Town B.

    How many miles is Town C from Town B? _____

11. A dessert at a restaurant contains 978 calories. That is 3 times the number of calories in one of its entrées.

    How many calories are in the entrée? _____

12. Kiki's garden is 336 square feet. That is 3 times the area of Matthew's garden.

    How many square feet is Matthew's garden? _____

Division Algorithm Without Remainders (C)

Practice Dividing by 1 Digit in Real-World Problems

Evaluate.

1. $240 - 128 \div 4 + 45$ _____

2. $56 \times 4 + 576 \div 8$ _____

3. $320 \div 5 - 204 \div 6$ _____

4. $125 + 78 \times 6 - 342 \div 9$ _____

5. $84 \div 3 \times 4 - 28$ _____

6. $162 \div 3 + 432 \div 9$ _____

Solve.

7. Aisha bakes 72 blueberry muffins. She packages them in boxes of 3 muffins each. She then sells each box for $5.

   a. How many boxes of muffins are there? _____

   b. Write an equation that can be used to solve for the amount of money Aisha earns from selling all the boxes of muffins. Let m represent the unknown value in your equation.

   _____

   c. How much money does Aisha earn from selling all the boxes of muffins?

   _____

8. Min's mother invites guests to a party. She invites 48 people from her side of the family, and she invites 64 people from her husband's side of the family. The tables for the guests fit 8 people each.

   a. How many people does Min's mother invite to the party? _____

   b. Write an equation to find the least number of tables Min's mother needs to seat her guests. Let t represent the unknown value in your equation.

   _____

   c. What is the least number of tables Min's mother needs to seat her guests?

   _____

9. James mixes 84 ounces of orange juice and 68 ounces of pineapple juice. He accidentally spills 32 ounces in the sink. He fills glasses that hold 6 ounces each with the remaining mixture.

   a. How many ounces of juice are in the mixture? _____

   b. How many ounces of the mixture are left after James spills 32 ounces? _____

   c. Write an equation to find the number of glasses James fills. Let g represent the unknown value in your equation.

   _____

   d. How many glasses does James fill? _____

Division is helpful to solve so many types of problems.

2-Digit by 1-Digit Division with Remainders (A)

Practice Dividing 2-Digit Numbers with Remainders Using Models

Solve.

1. These base-10 blocks model a division problem.

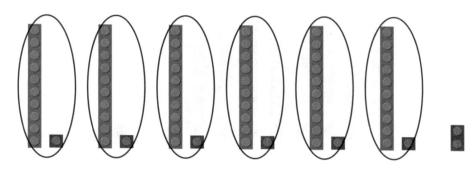

   a. Fill in the blanks: The model shows _____ base-10 blocks split into

   _____ groups. Each group has _____ blocks with

   _____ blocks left over.

   b. What division equation does this model represent?

   _____ ÷ _____ = _____ R _____

2. This area model represents a division problem.

	20	3
3	60	9

   2

   a. Fill in the blanks: The model shows a combined area of _____. The width of

   the rectangle is _____ and the length of the rectangle is _____.

   The square shows a remaining area of _____.

b. What division equation does this model represent?

_____ ÷ _____ = _____ R _____

Use the base-10 blocks to model the division problem. Then, find the quotient.

3. 84 ÷ 5 = _____ R _____

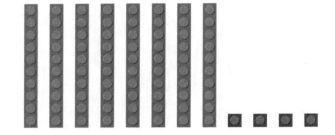

Complete the area model. Then, find the quotient.

4. 57 ÷ 4 = _____ R _____

	10		
4	___	16	___

5. 98 ÷ 9 = _____ R _____

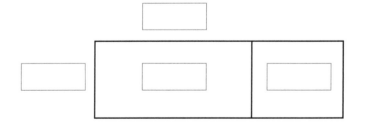

2-Digit by 1-Digit Division with Remainders (B)

Practice Dividing 2-Digit Numbers with Remainders

Divide the two-digit number by the one-digit number.

1. 8) 8 7   R ☐

    − ☐
    ___
      7

2. 6) 7 5   R ☐

    − ☐
    ___
      1 5

    − ☐
    ___
      ☐

3. 6) 8 9   R ☐

4. 3) 4 6   R ☐

5. $58 \div 9 =$ _____ R _____

6. $81 \div 4 =$ _____ R _____

7. $9\overline{)\ 6\ 7}$ R ☐

8. $3\overline{)\ 5\ 3}$ R ☐

9. $92 \div 5 =$ _____ R _____

10. $81 \div 7 =$ _____ R _____

11. $4\overline{)\ 7\ 3}$ R ☐

12. $73 \div 3 =$ _____ R _____

3-Digit by 1-Digit Division with Remainders (A)

Practice Dividing 3-Digit Numbers with Remainders Using Models

Solve.

1. This area model represents $343 \div 8$.

	40	2	
8	320	16	7

What is the solution?

$343 \div 8 =$ _____ R _____

2. This area model represents a division problem.

	100	3	
4	400	12	2

a. The dividend is the total area inside the rectangle. What is the total area inside the rectangle? _____

b. The divisor is the width of the rectangle. What is the width of the rectangle? _____

c. What division problem is shown in the model?

_____ ÷ _____

d. What is the solution to the division problem?

_____ R _____

Complete the area model. Then, find the quotient.

3. $527 \div 3 =$ _____ R _____

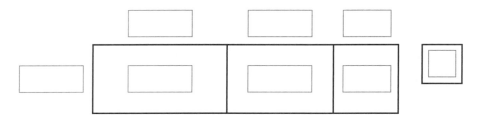

4. $764 \div 5 =$ _____ R _____

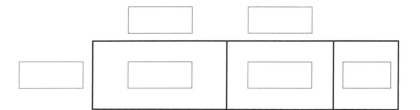

5. $469 \div 8 =$ _____ R _____

> Dividing makes sense with area models.

3-Digit by 1-Digit Division with Remainders (B)

Practice Dividing 3-Digit Numbers with Remainders

Divide the three-digit number by the one-digit number.

1. $6\overline{)\ 1\ 8\ 7}$ R ☐

2. $5\overline{)\ 7\ 6\ 4}$ R ☐

3. $3\overline{)\ 9\ 9\ 7}$ R ☐

4. $8\overline{)\ 2\ 0\ 4}$ R ☐

5. $830 \div 6 =$ _____ R _____

6. $411 \div 4 =$ _____ R _____

7. $9\overline{)646}$ ☐ R ☐

8. $3\overline{)286}$ ☐ R ☐

9. $391 \div 7 =$ _____ R _____

10. $747 \div 4 =$ _____ R _____

11. $5\overline{)622}$ ☐ R ☐

12. $800 \div 7 =$ _____ R _____

Practice Interpreting Remainders in Problem Solving

Answer the questions.

1. Sophia is selling bags of cookies at a bake sale. She bakes 147 cookies. She puts 4 cookies into each bag.

   a. What is $147 \div 4$? _____

   b. How many bags of 4 cookies does Sophia have? _____

   c. How many cookies are left over? _____

   d. Explain how you used the quotient of $147 \div 4$ to answer Part (b) and Part (c).

   _____

   _____

   _____

2. A group of 52 people are touring a museum. There is a maximum of 8 people in each tour group.

   a. What is $52 \div 8$? _____

   b. How many tour groups are needed for the 52 people?

   _____

   c. Explain how you used the quotient of $52 \div 8$ to answer Part (b).

   _____

   _____

3. Lena has 148 beads to make bracelets. Each bracelet uses 9 beads. Lena divides 148 by 9 and gets a quotient of 16 R4. Explain what the remainder of 4 means in terms of the problem.

_____

_____

Solve.

4. There are 38 people sitting at picnic tables. Each picnic table holds 6 people.

   If as many people sit at a table as possible, how many people are

   sitting at a table that is not full? _____

5. Shamika buys 112 ounces of cat food. Her cat eats 5 ounces of food each day.

   In how many days will Shamika need to buy more food? _____

6. Colin is making muffins. Each batch of muffins uses 2 cups of blueberries. Colin has 19 cups of blueberries.

   If he makes as many batches as he can, how many cups of blueberries

   will be left over? _____

7. A group of 57 people are going rafting. Each raft holds 6 people.

   How many rafts are needed? _____

8. Sienna orders pizzas for a party. Each pizza has 8 slices. There are 15 people at the party, and each person gets 2 slices.

   What is the fewest number of pizzas Sienna can order to feed

   all 15 people? _____

Problem Solving Using Division with Remainders (B)

Practice Solving Division Problems with Multiplicative Comparisons

Answer the questions.

1. Annie picks 23 pounds of apples. Her sister picks 9 pounds of apples.

    About how many times more pounds of apples does Annie pick than her sister?

    a. Write a multiplication equation that you can use to solve the problem.

    _____

    b. What is the related division equation? _____

    c. What is the solution to the problem? Show your work.
        Then, explain your answer in a complete sentence.

    _____

    _____

    d. What does the remainder part of the quotient tell you?

    _____

    _____

2. On Sunday, 458 people attend a play. This number is about 3 times the number of people who attend the play on Saturday.

    What is a reasonable estimate for how many people attend the play on Saturday? Justify your answer.

    _____

    _____

Solve.

3. Jace spends $237 for a camera. This amount is about 6 times as much as he spends for a baseball glove.

   About how much does the baseball glove cost?

   _____

4. Dylan is about twice as tall as Maria. Dylan is 73 inches tall.

   About how tall is Maria? _____

5. The table shows the highest and lowest temperatures ever recorded for different cities in Florida.

Record Temperatures for Florida Cities		
City	Highest temperature (°F)	Lowest temperature (°F)
Jacksonville	103	7
Tallahassee	105	6
Pensacola	106	5
Panama City	102	2

PlantMaps 2018

How many times greater is the record high temperature than the record low temperature for each city?

Jacksonville: _____

Tallahassee: _____

Pensacola: _____

Panama City: _____

Problem Solving Using Division with Remainders (C)

Practice Solving Problems Using Division with Remainders

Answer the questions.

1. A museum is open for 8 hours each day. A 7-minute movie at the visitors' center plays over and over while the museum is open.

   How many times does the entire movie play each day?

   a. Explain what steps you need to take to solve the problem.

   _____

   _____

   _____

   b. There are 60 minutes in 1 hour. How many minutes is the museum open each day? Show your work. Then, explain your answer in a complete sentence.

   _____

   _____

   c. What is the solution to the problem? Show your work. Then, explain your answer in a complete sentence.

   _____

   _____

   d. What does the remainder part of the quotient tell you?

   _____

   _____

2. A photographer has 19 black-and-white pictures and 22 color pictures. He displays the pictures on a wall in 4 rows.

   a. How many pictures are in each row? _____

   b. How many pictures are left over? _____

   c. Check your answer to justify the solution.

   _____

   _____

Solve.

3. Damian bakes 125 cookies. This number is about 4 times as many cookies as Sharona bakes.

   About how many cookies does Sharona bake? _____

4. The table shows how many people different sizes of canoes hold. A group of 19 children and 12 adults want to rent canoes.

   a. How many canoes will they need if all the canoes they rent are double canoes?

   _____

   b. How many canoes will they need if all the canoes they rent are triple canoes?

   _____

   c. How many canoes will they need if they rent the fewest possible number of canoes?

   _____

Canoe Sizes	
Size	Number of people
single	1
double	2
triple	3
family	4

Denominators of 10 and 100 (A)

Practice Working with Fractions with Denominators 10 and 100

Write a fraction with a denominator of 100 that is equivalent to the given fraction.

1.

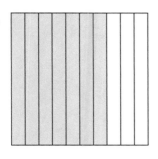 =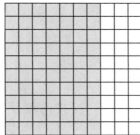

$$\frac{7}{10} = \underline{\hspace{2cm}}$$

2. $\frac{1}{10} = \underline{\hspace{2cm}}$ 3. $\frac{8}{10} = \underline{\hspace{2cm}}$

4. $\frac{5}{10} = \underline{\hspace{2cm}}$ 5. $\frac{9}{10} = \underline{\hspace{2cm}}$

6. $\frac{4}{10} = \underline{\hspace{2cm}}$ 7. $\frac{6}{10} = \underline{\hspace{2cm}}$

8. $\frac{2}{10} = \underline{\hspace{2cm}}$ 9. $\frac{3}{10} = \underline{\hspace{2cm}}$

Add. Express your answer as a fraction with a denominator of 100.

10.

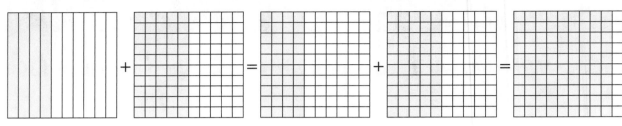

$$\frac{4}{10} \quad + \quad \frac{50}{100} \quad = \underline{\hspace{1.5cm}} + \quad \frac{50}{100} \quad = \underline{\hspace{1.5cm}}$$

Add. Express your answer in simplest form.

11. $\frac{3}{10} + \frac{19}{100} = \underline{\hspace{2cm}}$

12. $\frac{8}{10} + \frac{5}{100} = \underline{\hspace{2cm}}$

13. $\frac{28}{100} + \frac{2}{10} = \underline{\hspace{2cm}}$

14. $\frac{46}{100} + \frac{6}{10} = \underline{\hspace{2cm}}$

With a little practice, I can add fractions with denominators of 10 and 100.

Denominators of 10 and 100 (B)

Practice Reading and Writing Decimals Through Hundredths

Write a fraction and a decimal to describe the portion of the model that is shaded.

1.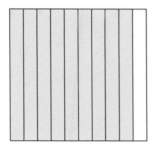

    fraction: _____

    decimal: _____

2.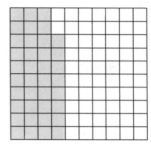

    fraction: _____

    decimal: _____

Write a decimal equivalent to the given fraction.

3. $\frac{5}{10} =$ _____

4. $\frac{4}{100} =$ _____

5. $5\frac{3}{10} =$ _____

6. $\frac{60}{100} =$ _____

7. $\frac{78}{100} =$ _____

8. $10\frac{6}{100} =$ _____

9. $5\frac{26}{100} =$ _____

10. $24\frac{1}{10} =$ _____

Write the number form of the decimal.

11. three-tenths _____

12. five-hundredths _____

13. eight and four-tenths _____

14. two and fifteen-hundredths _____

15. nine and four-hundredths _____

Write the word form of the decimal.

16. 0.07 _____

17. 0.5 _____

18. 0.18 _____

19. 5.4 _____

20. 6.30 _____

Denominators of 10 and 100 (C)

Practice Writing Decimals as Fractions

Fill in the blanks to complete the statement.

1. Since 0.3 is _____ tenths, 0.3 can be written as the fraction _____.

2. Since 0.07 is _____ hundredths, 0.07 can be written as the fraction

   _____.

3. Since 2.7 is 2 and _____ tenths, 2.7 can be written as the mixed

   number _____.

4. Since 4.29 is 4 and _____ hundredths, 4.29 can be written as the mixed

   number _____.

Write the decimal as an equivalent fraction or mixed number in simplest form.

5. 0.1 _____   6. 0.39 _____

7. 0.6 _____   8. 1.8 _____

9. 0.04 _____

10. 0.22 _____

11. 9.4 _____

12. 8.47 _____

13. 2.35 _____

14. 0.2 _____

15. 4.06 _____

16. 0.9 _____

17. 3.41 _____

18. 8.45 _____

19. 10.6 _____

20. 14.18 _____

Comparing Decimals (A)

Practice Comparing and Ordering Decimals

Compare the numbers using the models and <, >, or =.

1. 0.5 ☐ 0.7

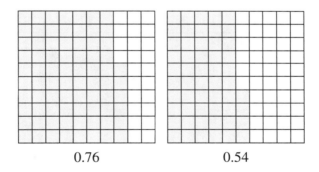

0.5   0.7

2. 0.76 ☐ 0.54

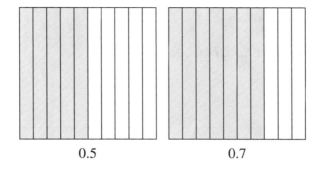

0.76   0.54

3. 0.48 ☐ 0.6

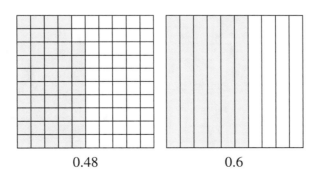

0.48   0.6

Compare the numbers using <, >, or =.

4. 0.79 ☐ 0.7

5. 0.18 ☐ 0.26

6. 0.2 ☐ 0.20

7. 0.46 ☐ 0.5

8. 0.8 ☐ 0.57

Order the numbers from least to greatest.

9. 0.44, 0.4, 1, 0.36 _____

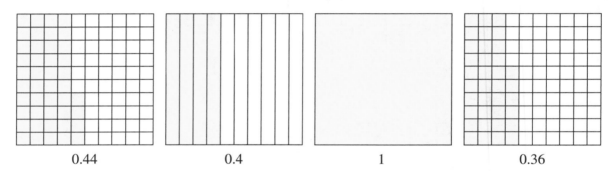

0.44   0.4   1   0.36

10. 0.16, 0.1, 0.2, 0.18 _____

11. 0.36, 0.3, 0.25, 0.31 _____

12. 0.94, 0.9, 1.2, 1 _____

13. 3.2, 3.11, 3.08, 3.21 _____

14. 4.03, 4.1, 4, 4.01 _____

15. 0.08, 0, 0.02, 1 _____

Comparing Decimals (B)

Practice Working with Decimals Using a Number Line

Plot and label the number on the number line.

1. 0.7

2. 3.54

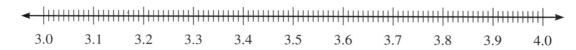

Write the coordinate of the given point.

3. _____

4. _____

5. _____

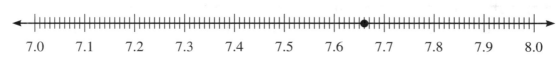

Plot and label each number on the number line. Then, compare the numbers using <, >, or =.

6. 1.8 ☐ 1.48

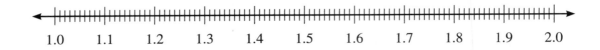

1.0   1.1   1.2   1.3   1.4   1.5   1.6   1.7   1.8   1.9   2.0

7. 4.25 ☐ 4.55

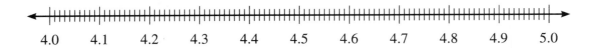

4.0   4.1   4.2   4.3   4.4   4.5   4.6   4.7   4.8   4.9   5.0

8. 6.4 ☐ 6.40

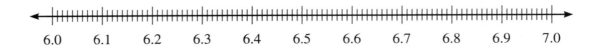

6.0   6.1   6.2   6.3   6.4   6.5   6.6   6.7   6.8   6.9   7.0

Plot and label each number on the number line. Then, order the numbers from least to greatest.

9. 3.17, 3.63, 4, 3.41 _____

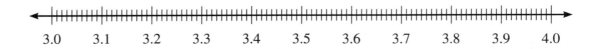

3.0   3.1   3.2   3.3   3.4   3.5   3.6   3.7   3.8   3.9   4.0

10. 0.69, 0, 0.36, 0.05 _____

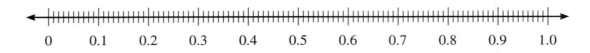

0   0.1   0.2   0.3   0.4   0.5   0.6   0.7   0.8   0.9   1.0

Units of Length (A)

Practice Working with Metric Units of Length

Fill in the blanks to complete the statement.

1. 5 meters = 5 × _____ centimeters = _____ centimeters

2. 3 kilometers = 3 × _____ meters = _____ meters

3. 9 meters = 9 × _____ centimeters = _____ centimeters

4. 12 kilometers = 12 × _____ meters = _____ meters

Determine whether the statement is True or False.

5. A kilometer is larger than a meter. _____

6. A centimeter is larger than a meter. _____

7. A centimeter is smaller than a kilometer. _____

I can stretch my arms about a meter wide.

Answer the question.

8. Eloise plants a sunflower that grows 2 meters tall.

   How tall is the sunflower in centimeters? _____ centimeters

9. Min and his friends enter a 4-kilometer race to raise money for the local food bank.

   How long is the race in meters? _____ meters

Complete the table.

10. Change kilometers to meters.

Kilometers	Meters
2	
6	
10	
13	

11. Change meters to centimeters.

Meters	Centimeters
3	
6	
8	
12	

Units of Length (B)

Practice Working with U.S. Customary Units of Length

Fill in the blanks to complete the statement.

1. 4 yards = 4 × _____ feet = _____ feet

2. 2 feet = 2 × _____ inches = _____ inches

3. 11 yards = 11 × _____ feet = _____ feet

4. 10 feet = 10 × _____ inches = _____ inches

Determine whether the statement is True or False.

5. An inch is larger than a foot. _____

6. A yard is larger than an inch. _____

7. A foot is smaller than a yard. _____

I can draw an inch on my pad but not a foot and definitely not a yard!

Answer the question.

8. The public pool in James's neighborhood is 30 yards long.

   How long is the pool in feet? _____ feet

9. Kiki uses a 6-foot ladder to reach a high shelf.

   How tall is the ladder in inches? _____ inches

Complete the table.

10. Change yards to feet.

Yards	Feet
8	
13	
20	
32	

11. Change feet to inches.

Feet	Inches
4	
6	
9	
12	

Units of Mass and Weight (A)

Practice Working with Metric Units of Mass

Fill in the blanks to complete the statement.

1. A kilogram is equal to _____ grams. Therefore, a kilogram is

   _____ times larger than a gram.

2. 2 kilograms = 2 × _____ grams = _____ grams

3. 33 kilograms = 33 × _____ grams = _____ grams

4. 9 kilograms = 9 × _____ grams = _____ grams

5. 14 kilograms = _____ grams

6. 21 kilograms = _____ grams

7. 7 kilograms = _____ grams

Answer the question.

8. Maria grows a pumpkin with a mass of 6 kilograms.

   How many grams is the pumpkin? _____ grams

9. Jada buys a bushel of apples with a mass of 18 kilograms.

   How heavy is the bushel of apples in grams? _____ grams

Complete the table.

10. Change kilograms to grams.

Kilograms	Grams
8	
11	
14	
24	

I always multiply to change a larger unit to a smaller unit.

Units of Mass and Weight (B)

Practice Working with U.S. Customary Units of Weight

Fill in the blanks to complete the statement.

1. A pound is equal to _____ ounces. Therefore, a pound is

   _____ times larger than an ounce.

2. 2 pounds = 2 × _____ ounces = _____ ounces

3. 7 pounds = 7 × _____ ounces = _____ ounces

4. 20 pounds = 20 × _____ ounces = _____ ounces

5. 9 pounds = _____ ounces

6. 14 pounds = _____ ounces

7. 16 pounds = _____ ounces

Answer the question.

8. Jada buys an 8-pound bag of dog food.

    How many ounces does it weigh? _____ ounces

9. James's new laptop weighs about 5 pounds.

    How many ounces does the laptop weigh? about _____ ounces

Complete the table.

10. Change pounds to ounces.

Pounds	Ounces
4	
6	
10	
12	

Units of Volume (A)

Practice Working with Metric Units of Volume

Fill in the blanks to complete the statement.

1. A liter is equal to _____ milliliters. Therefore, a liter is

   _____ times larger than a milliliter.

2. 5 liters = 5 × _____ milliliters = _____ milliliters

3. 8 liters = 8 × _____ milliliters = _____ milliliters

4. 35 liters = 35 × _____ milliliters = _____ milliliters

5. 16 liters = _____ milliliters

6. 9 liters = _____ milliliters

7. 27 liters = _____ milliliters

Answer the question.

8. Amelie has a watering can that holds 3 liters of water.

   How many milliliters of water does the watering can hold? _____ milliliters

9. Raj makes an indoor fountain. He fills the fountain with 12 liters of water.

   How many milliliters of water does the fountain hold? _____ milliliters

Complete the table.

10. Change liters to milliliters.

Liters	Milliliters
4	
6	
10	
12	

I hope my watering can has enough milliliters of water for all of these flowers.

Units of Volume (B)

Practice Working with U.S. Customary Units of Volume

Fill in the blanks to complete the statements.

1. What are the relationships between cups, pints, quarts, and gallons?

   a. 1 pint = _____ cups

   b. 1 quart = _____ pints = _____ cups

   c. 1 gallon = _____ quarts = _____ pints = _____ cups

   d. A pint is _____ times larger than a cup.

   e. A quart is _____ times larger than a pint and _____ times larger than a cup.

   f. A gallon is _____ times larger than a quart, _____ times larger than a pint, and _____ times larger than a cup.

2. 5 gallons = 5 × _____ quarts = _____ quarts

3. 7 quarts = 7 × _____ pints = _____ pints

4. 10 pints = 10 × _____ cups = _____ cups

5. 3 quarts = 3 × _____ cups = _____ cups

Answer the question.

6. Maria has a watering can that holds 3 pints of water.

   How many cups of water does the watering can hold? _____ cups

7. Raj sets up an aquarium that holds 20 gallons of water.

   How many quarts of water does the aquarium hold? _____ quarts

8. Min mixes 1 quart of orange juice, 2 quarts of apple juice, and 1 quart of grape juice to make a fruit punch.

   a. How many quarts of juice does Min use? _____ quarts

   b. How many pints of juice does Min use? _____ pints

Complete the table.

9. Change the larger units of volume to smaller units of volume.

Larger units	Smaller units
9 gallons	quarts
12 pints	cups
11 quarts	pints
5 quarts	cups

Units of Time (A)

Practice Comparing Units of Time

Fill in the blank to complete the statement.

1. There are 60 seconds in 1 _____ .

2. A minute is _____ times longer than a second.

3. There are _____ minutes in 1 hour.

4. An hour is _____ times longer than a minute.

Compare using <, >, or =.

5. 1 hour _____ 1 minute

6. 1 minute _____ 1 second

7. 1 hour _____ 60 minutes

8. 1 minute _____ 60 seconds

9. 1 second _____ 1 hour

Sixty seconds sounds like a lot longer than 1 minute, but I know they are really the same.

Answer the question.

10. Matthew says that 60 seconds and 1 hour are the same length of time. Is Mathew correct? Explain.

_____

_____

_____

11. Does it take closer to a minute or a second to snap your fingers? Explain.

_____

_____

_____

12. Does it take closer to a minute or an hour to get ready for school in the morning? Explain.

_____

_____

_____

13. Does it take closer to an hour, a minute, or a second to drink a glass of water? Explain.

_____

_____

_____

Practice Converting Units of Time

Fill in the blanks to complete the statement.

1. To convert from hours to minutes, multiply the number of

   _____ by _____ minutes.

2. 2 hours = 2 × _____ minutes = _____ minutes

3. To convert from minutes to seconds, multiply the number of _____

   by _____ seconds.

4. 4 minutes = 4 × _____ seconds = _____ seconds

5. 5 hours = _____ minutes

6. 10 hours = _____ minutes

7. 6 minutes = _____ seconds

8. 11 minutes = _____ seconds

Answer the question.

9. Aisha and Eric are on a 3-hour bicycle ride.

   How many minutes does their ride take? _____ minutes

10. Matthew makes some cookies. He bakes them for 12 minutes.

   How many seconds does Matthew bake the cookies for? _____ seconds

Complete the table.

11. Change hours to minutes.

Hours	Minutes
4	
6	
9	
13	

12. Change minutes to seconds.

Minutes	Seconds
3	
7	
8	
15	

Word Problems with Measurements (A)

Practice Representing Measurements

Solve.

1. Adam has 128 fluid ounces of milk. He drinks 16 fluid ounces of milk each day.

   How many fluid ounces of milk are left after 4 days?

   a. Let m represent the unknown in this problem. What does the problem ask you to find?

   _____

   _____

   b. Describe in words how you could solve the problem.

   _____

   _____

   _____

   c. Write an equation that can be used to find the value of m.

   _____

Write an equation that can be used to solve the problem. Do not solve the problem.

2. Pedro runs 25 kilometers each week.

   How many kilometers does Pedro run in 12 weeks?

   _____

3. Caleb weighs 18 pounds less than 3 times what his brother Liam weighs. Liam weighs 65 pounds.

   How much does Caleb weigh?

   _____

Use the information in the table to write an equation that can be used to answer the question. Do not solve the equation.

4. The table shows the wingspans of different butterflies.

Butterfly	Wingspan (in.)
black swallowtail	$3\frac{5}{10}$
monarch	$3\frac{7}{10}$
queen	$2\frac{4}{10}$
western tailed blue	$\frac{7}{10}$

National Park Service 2015

a. How much greater is the black swallowtail's wingspan than the western tailed blue's wingspan?

   _____

b. How much less is the monarch's wingspan than the black swallowtail's and western tailed blue's wingspans combined?

   _____

Word Problems with Measurements (B)

Practice Solving Distance Problems

Solve.

1. At the beginning of the year, Tonya was 54 inches tall. At the end of the year she is $56\frac{1}{2}$ inches tall.

   How many inches does Tonya grow during the year?

   a. Let i represent the unknown in this problem. What does the problem ask you to find?

   _____

   _____

   b. Describe in words how you can solve the problem.

   _____

   _____

   c. Write an equation that can be used to find the value of i.

   _____

   d. How many inches does Tonya grow during the year? _____

2. Duncan walks 14 kilometers each week. How many kilometers does he walk in 15 weeks? _____

3. A football field is 120 yards long. How many feet long is the football field? _____

4. A rectangular swimming pool is 20 feet long. The width of the pool is 96 inches less than the length.

   How many inches wide is the pool? _____

5. The table shows snowfall amounts for different days.

Day	Snowfall (cm)
Monday	$16\frac{3}{5}$
Tuesday	$3\frac{2}{5}$
Wednesday	$7\frac{1}{5}$
Thursday	$4\frac{4}{5}$

   a. How much snow fell on Monday and Tuesday combined? _____

   b. How much more snow fell on Thursday than on Tuesday? _____

   c. How much more snow fell on Monday than on Thursday? _____

6. A sign says that you must be 38 inches to ride the carousel at an amusement park. Juan is 4 feet tall.

   Is Juan tall enough to ride the carousel? Explain your answer.

   _____

   _____

   _____

7. A piece of string is 6 meters long. Cameron cuts the string into 8 equal pieces.

   How many centimeters long is each piece of string that Cameron cuts? _____

Word Problems with Measurements (C)

Practice Solving Weight Problems

Solve.

1. Jayla has a bag of dog food that weighs 30 pounds. Her dog eats 4 ounces of food twice a day.

   How many days will the dog food last?

   a. The weight of the bag of food is given in pounds. The amount Jayla's dog eats at each meal is given in ounces. So, begin by converting 30 pounds to ounces. There are 16 ounces in a pound.

   30 lb = _____ oz

   b. Write an expression to show how many ounces of food

   Jayla's dog eats each day. _____

   c. How many ounces of food does Jayla's dog eat each day? _____

   d. What operation can you use to find how many days the food

   will last? _____

   e. What expression can you use to solve the problem? _____

   f. How many days will the dog food last? _____

2. Jane buys $\frac{3}{4}$ pound of apples. How many ounces of apples does she

   buy? Use the number line to solve the problem. _____

3. A porcupine weighs 2 kilograms. How many grams does the porcupine weigh? _____

4. Jason weighs 3 times as much as his sister. Jason weighs 93 pounds.

   How much does his sister weigh in pounds? _____

5. The table shows the typical weights of different breeds of dogs.

Dog breed	Weight (lb)
Afghan hound	55
beagle	15
Irish wolfhound	120
Pekingese	8

AKC Staff 2017

   a. How many more pounds does an Irish wolfhound weigh than a beagle? _____

   b. How many times greater is an Irish wolfhound's weight than

      a Pekingese's weight? _____

   c. How much does a Pekingese weigh in ounces? _____

   d. How many ounces less does a beagle weigh than an Afghan hound? _____

6. Sachi buys 5 pounds of pizza dough to make pizzas. Each pizza uses
   9 ounces of dough.

   What is the greatest number of pizzas Sachi can make with the dough? _____

7. Sharonna picks 925 grams of strawberries. She uses 275 grams of
   strawberries to make a tart and 372 grams to make a cake.

   How many grams of strawberries does Sharonna have left? _____

Word Problems with Measurements (D)

Practice Solving Liquid Volume Problems

Solve.

1. Casey has a pitcher containing 3 liters of water. She drinks 250 milliliters of water with her breakfast and 500 milliliters of water with her lunch. At dinner, she drinks 425 milliliters of water.

   How many milliliters of water does Casey have left in the pitcher?

   a. Convert the number of liters of water in the pitcher to milliliters.

      3 L = _____ mL

   b. Write an equation that can be used to solve the problem. Let w represent the number of milliliters of water left in the pitcher.

      _____

      _____

   c. How many milliliters of water are left in the pitcher? _____

2. Lana makes 4 quarts of cranberry punch and 3 quarts of pineapple punch. How many cups of punch does Lana make? Use the diagram to help you solve the problem.

1 gallon							
1 quart		1 quart		1 quart		1 quart	
1 pint	1 pint	1 pint	1 pint	1 pint	1 pint	1 pint	1 pint
1 cup 1 cup	1 cup 1 cup	1 cup 1 cup	1 cup 1 cup	1 cup 1 cup	1 cup 1 cup	1 cup 1 cup	1 cup 1 cup

_____

3. Josie makes peanut butter sandwiches. She uses $\frac{1}{8}$ cup of peanut butter on each sandwich.

   How many cups of peanut butter does Josie need for 9 sandwiches? _____

4. There are 200 milliliters of juice in a juice box. How many milliliters of

   juice are in 8 juice boxes? _____

5. A small mug contains $1\frac{1}{2}$ cups of coffee. A large mug contains $2\frac{1}{2}$ cups of coffee. Deanna orders 2 large coffees and 1 small coffee.

   How many cups of coffee does Deanna order? _____

6. Tamiko has a fish tank that holds 30 gallons of water. Jasmine has a fish tank that holds 25 gallons of water.

   How many more quarts of water does Tamiko's fish tank hold? _____

7. Charlotte is making cornbread. The recipe calls for 1 cup of buttermilk. Charlotte has one measuring cup that hold 4 cups and another that holds 3 cups.

   How can Charlotte use the two measuring cups she has to measure exactly 1 cup of buttermilk?

   _____

   _____

   _____

   _____

   _____

Word Problems with Time and Money (A)

Practice Solving Money Problems

Solve.

1. Xavier buys a dog collar that costs $6.79. He pays for the dog collar with a $10 bill.

    How much change does Xavier receive?

    a. Draw a diagram you can use to count up to find the change.

    b. How much change does Xavier receive? _____

2. How much money is shown?

    _____

3. Dylan buys 2 boxes of trading cards. Each box costs $18.

    How much does Dylan spend in all? _____

4. Cheyenne saved $8 last month and $9 this month. She uses the money she saved to buy a T-shirt that costs $11.

How much money does Cheyenne have left? _____

5. Dontrelle buys a model car that costs $16. He pays for the car with four $5 bills.

How much change does Dontrelle receive? _____

6. The table shows the costs of pizzas by size.

   a. Jason buys 2 mini pizzas and 1 small pizza.

   How much do Jason's pizzas cost? _____

   b. Dana buys 4 large pizzas and 1 mini pizza.

   How much do Dana's pizzas cost? _____

   c. Asra buys 2 small pizzas and 1 mini pizza. She pays for the pizzas with a $20 bill.

   How much change does Asra receive? _____

Pizza size	Cost
mini	$5
small	$7
medium	$9
large	$13

7. Caitlyn buys a sandwich and a drink for lunch. The cost of each item is shown.

Sandwich Cost

Drink Cost

How much does Caitlyn spend in all? _____

Word Problems with Time and Money (B)

Practice Solving Time Problems

Solve.

1. Mae is going on vacation. She drives 3 hours and 45 minutes in the morning and 2 hours and 30 minutes in the afternoon.

   Use the number line to find how many hours and minutes she drives in all.

   _____

2. Jemma starts reading at the time shown on the clock. She reads for 1 hour and 15 minutes.

   What time does Jemma stop reading? _____

3. Rosita boards the train at 11:55 a.m. She gets off the train at 4:34 p.m.

   How long is Rosita's train ride? _____

4. Jax takes a bus from Washington, D.C., to New York City. The trip takes 5 hours and 47 minutes. He arrives in New York City at 1:58 p.m.

   What time did the bus leave Washington, D.C.? _____

5. The table shows the departure times of different boat rides. A boat ride takes 27 minutes.

Boat Rides	
Boat name	**Departure time**
Bounty	9:52 a.m.
Sea Mist	11:38 a.m.
Smooth Sailor	2:05 p.m.
Ocean Flyer	4:46 p.m.

a. Carlotta takes a boat ride on the *Bounty*.

   What time does her ride end? _____

b. Dan takes a boat ride on the *Ocean Flyer*.

   What time does his boat ride end? _____

c. Erin misses the *Bounty* boat ride. She wants to take the next boat

   ride. How long does she have to wait? _____

6. Jerry records the time it takes him to do 25 push-ups. He records his time for different days in the table in minutes and seconds.

   Complete the table by finding each time in seconds.

Day	Time in minutes and seconds	Time in seconds
Monday	2 minutes and 38 seconds	
Thursday	2 minutes and 22 seconds	
Sunday	2 minutes and 8 seconds	

Measurements and Line Plots (A)

Practice Representing Data on a Line Plot

Answer the questions.

1. The line plot shows the ages of the members in a chorus.

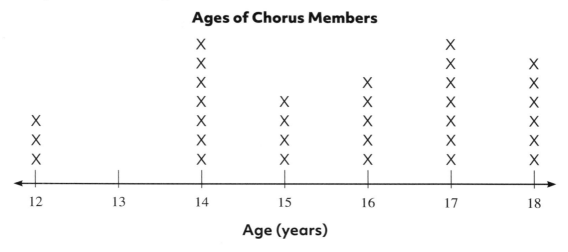

Ages of Chorus Members

Age (years)

a. How many people are in the chorus? _____

b. How old is the oldest person in the chorus? _____

c. How many people in the chorus are 14 years old? _____

d. There are no Xs above the number 13. What does this mean?

_____

e. How many more 16-year-old members are in the chorus than

12-year-old members? _____

f. How many people in the chorus are younger than 16? _____

g. For which ages are there more than 5 people in the chorus?

_____

2. Make a line plot to represent the data. Then, use the line plot to answer the questions.

Nail Head Widths	
Width (in.)	Frequency
$\frac{1}{8}$	4
$\frac{1}{4}$	2
$\frac{3}{8}$	1
$\frac{1}{2}$	5
$\frac{5}{8}$	3
$\frac{3}{4}$	4
$\frac{7}{8}$	4
1	4

a. How many nail head widths are recorded in this line plot?

_____

b. What is the measurement of the widest nail head?

_____

c. How many nail heads are $\frac{5}{8}$ inch wide?

_____

d. How many nail heads are less than $\frac{1}{2}$ inch wide?

_____

3. Miriam teaches people how to play the piano. She surveys her students to find out how many hours each student practices the piano each day. The data are shown in this list.

$$1\frac{1}{2}, \frac{3}{4}, \frac{1}{2}, 1, 1, 1\frac{1}{4}, 1\frac{1}{2}, 1\frac{1}{2}, \frac{1}{4}, \frac{1}{2}, \frac{1}{2}, 1\frac{1}{2}, 1\frac{3}{4}, \frac{3}{4}, \frac{3}{4}, 1, \frac{3}{4}, \frac{1}{2}, \frac{1}{2}, \frac{3}{4}, 1, 1, 1\frac{1}{4}, \frac{3}{4}, 1\frac{1}{2}$$

a. Organize the data in a frequency table.

Number of hours	Frequency

I love math and singing!

b. Make a line plot to represent the data. Remember to give the line plot a title and to label the number line.

_____

0   $\frac{1}{4}$ $\frac{1}{2}$ $\frac{3}{4}$ 1 $1\frac{1}{4}$ $1\frac{1}{2}$ $1\frac{3}{4}$ 2

_____

c. Use the line plot to answer the questions.

- How many people does Miriam teach?

_____

- What is the greatest amount of time a student practices?

_____

- How many students practice for $\frac{3}{4}$ hour?

_____

- How many students practice longer than 1 hour?

_____

Measurements and Line Plots (B)

Practice Interpreting Data on a Line Plot Using Addition

Sander is a baker. He keeps track of the amount of cinnamon he uses each day for a week. Use the table and the line plot to answer each question.

Amount of Cinnamon Used	
Day	Amount (tablespoons)
Monday	$3\frac{3}{8}$
Tuesday	$3\frac{1}{8}$
Wednesday	$3\frac{1}{8}$
Thursday	$3\frac{2}{8}$
Friday	$3\frac{6}{8}$
Saturday	$4\frac{1}{8}$
Sunday	$4\frac{1}{8}$

Number of Days

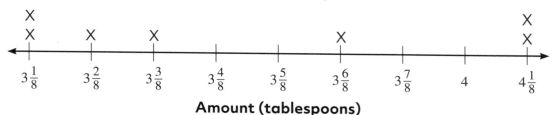

Amount (tablespoons)

1. How many days does Sander use $3\frac{4}{8}$ tablespoons of cinnamon? _____

2. What day or days does he use the most cinnamon? _____

3. What day or days does Sander use the least amount of cinnamon?

   _____

4. How many days does Sander use $4\frac{1}{8}$ tablespoons of cinnamon? _____

5. How much cinnamon does he use in all on Monday and Tuesday? _____

6. How much cinnamon does Sander use in all on the days he uses

   the most cinnamon? _____

7. How much cinnamon does he use in all on the days he uses
   $3\frac{1}{8}$ tablespoons of cinnamon and the days he uses $4\frac{1}{8}$ tablespoons

   of cinnamon? _____

8. How much cinnamon does Sander use in all on the days he uses greater
   than $3\frac{1}{8}$ tablespoons of cinnamon and less than $4\frac{1}{8}$ tablespoons of

   cinnamon? _____

9. Sander uses more cinnamon on each weekend day than he uses any
   day during the week. What could be the reason for this?

   _____

   _____

   _____

   _____

10. How much cinnamon does Sander use in all during the week? _____

Measurements and Line Plots (C)

Practice Interpreting Data on a Line Plot Using Subtraction

Amelie measures the insects that she has collected for her project.
The table and line plot show the lengths of the different insects.
Use the table and the line plot to answer the questions.

Lengths of Insects	
Insect	Length (in.)
cricket	$1\frac{6}{8}$
centipede	$2\frac{1}{8}$
bee	$1\frac{4}{8}$
beetle	$1\frac{7}{8}$
grasshopper	$1\frac{7}{8}$
wasp	$1\frac{4}{8}$
dragonfly	$2\frac{1}{8}$
cicada	$2\frac{1}{8}$

Number of Insects

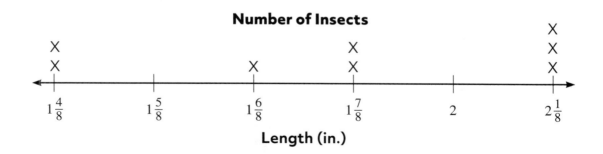

Length (in.)

1. How many insects are $2\frac{1}{8}$ inches long? _____

2. How much longer is a beetle than a bee? _____

3. How much longer is a centipede than a wasp? _____

4. What is the difference between the length of the longest insect and

   the length of the shortest insect? _____

5. How much shorter is a cricket than a dragonfly? _____

6. What is the difference between the length of the longest insect and

   the length of a bee? _____

7. What is the difference between the length of the insect that is

   $1\frac{6}{8}$ inches long and the length of the shortest insect? _____

8. What is the difference between the length of the longest

   insect and the length of the insect that is $1\frac{6}{8}$ inches long? _____

Studying insects is
a fun hobby.

Area and Perimeter Problems (A)

Practice Solving Problems Using Perimeters of Rectangles

Find the perimeter of the rectangle.

1. Complete the equations to find the perimeter of the rectangle.

$l = 41$ mm

$w = 29$ mm

$P = 2 \times l + 2 \times w$

$P = 2 \times \boxed{} + 2 \times \boxed{}$

$P = \boxed{} + \boxed{}$

$P = \boxed{}$

The perimeter is $\boxed{}$ millimeters.

2.
9 m

11 m

3.
48 ft

11 ft

4.
18 yd

28 yd

5.
31 mm

31 mm

6.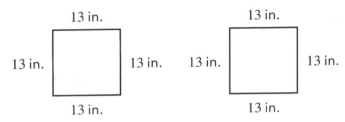

105 in.

45 in.

_____

7.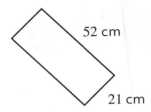

52 cm

21 cm

_____

Solve.

8. Trudy sews together two quilt squares like the ones shown. She then puts fringe around the outside of the new rectangular piece of material.

13 in.

13 in. 13 in.

13 in.

13 in.

13 in. 13 in.

13 in.

How many inches of fringe does Trudy use? _____

9. A park is shaped like a square with sides that are 729 yards long.

What is the length of a bike path that goes along the entire outside

perimeter of the park? _____

10. Ari says the formula $P = 2 \times l + 2 \times w$ can be used to find the perimeter of a rectangle. Shauna says the formula $P = l + l + w + w$ should be used. Dione says the formula is $P = 2 \times (l + w)$.

Who is correct? Explain your answer.

_____

_____

_____

_____

Area and Perimeter Problems (B)

Practice Solving Problems Using Areas of Rectangles

Find the area of the rectangle.

1. Complete the equations to find the area of the rectangle.

$l = 15$ cm

$w = 9$ cm

$A = l \times w$

$A = \boxed{} \times \boxed{}$

$A = \boxed{}$

The area is $\boxed{}$ square centimeters.

2.

15 ft

21 ft

_____

3.

9 ft

5 ft

_____

4.

11 yd

22 yd

_____

5.

25 mm

25 mm

_____

6.

86 yd

24 yd

_____

7.

30 in.

15 in.

_____

Solve.

8. Briana helps her mother make a quilt. The quilt is 6 feet wide and 12 feet long.

What is the area of the quilt? _____

9. Use the rectangle to answer the questions.

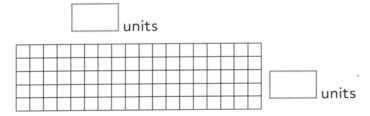

☐ units

☐ units

a. Find the length and width of the rectangle.

b. Describe two ways to find the area of the rectangle.

_____

_____

_____

c. What is the area of the rectangle? _____

10. Find the area of a rectangle that is 21 yards long by 9 yards wide. _____

11. Sam makes a rectangular banner. The width of the banner is 8 inches less than its length. The width is 48 inches.

What is the area of the banner? _____

Area and Perimeter Problems (C)

Practice Finding Unknown Lengths of Rectangles

Find the unknown side length of the rectangle.

1. This rectangle has an area of 176 square centimeters. Complete the equations to find the unknown side length of this rectangle.

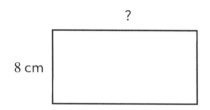

?

8 cm

$A = l \times w$

$\boxed{} = l \times \boxed{}$

$l = \boxed{} \div \boxed{}$

$l = \boxed{}$

The unknown side length is $\boxed{}$ centimeters.

2.

10 m

?

$A = 40 \text{ m}^2$

? = _____

3.

?

2 ft

$P = 34 \text{ ft}$

? = _____

4.

?

6 m

$A = 42 \text{ m}^2$

? = _____

5.

7 ft

?

$P = 26 \text{ ft}$

? = _____

6.

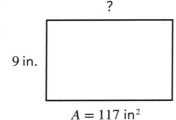

? = _____

7.

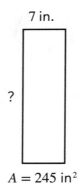

? = _____

Solve.

8. The tablecloth has a perimeter of 240 inches.

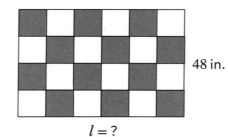

How long is the tablecloth? _____

9. A square has a perimeter of 220 millimeters.

   a. Describe how you can find the length of each side of the square.

   _____

   _____

   _____

   b. What is the length of each side of the square? _____

10. The area of a floor is 162 square feet. The length of the floor is 18 feet.

   What is the width of the floor? _____

Exploring Larger Numbers (A)

Practice Understanding Relationships Among Place Values

Solve.

1. Rami states that the value of the digit 4 in 149,832 is 10 times the value of the digit 4 in 384,923.

   a. What is the value of the digit 4 in 384,923? _____

   b. What is 10 times the value of the digit 4 in 384,923? _____

   c. What is the value of the digit 4 in 149,832? _____

   d. Is Rami correct? Explain.

   _____

   _____

   _____

   _____

2. For each number, explain whether the digit 9 is 10 times the value of the digit 9 in 168,932.

   a. 294,733

   _____

   _____

   _____

   _____

b. 439,023

_____

_____

_____

c. 938,120

_____

_____

3. Jessica writes the number 178,392. Kiki wants to write another number so that the digit 7 has a value that is 10 times greater than the digit 7 in Jessica's number.

In what place value should the digit 7 appear in Kiki's number? _____

4. Write a number that includes the digit 7. Let the digit 7 have a value that is 10 times the value of the digit 7 in 14,738.

_____

5. Write a number that includes the digit 6. Let the digit 6 have the same value as the digit 6 in 57,863.

_____

6. Circle the numbers in which the digit 1 has the same value as the digit 1 in 231,849.

821,902   12,930   31,392   1,098   102,398   293,198

7. Circle the numbers in which the digit 3 has a value that is 10 times the value as the digit 3 in 193,874.

32,892   304,896   123,486   278,398   234,473   38,216

Practice Rounding Multidigit Whole Numbers Up to 1 Million

Use the number line to round the number to the given place value.

1. 64,382 to the nearest ten thousand _____

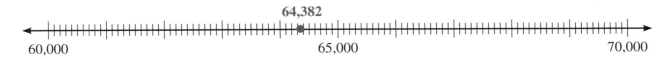

2. 854,392 to the nearest hundred thousand _____

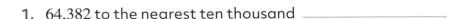

3. 738,035 to the nearest ten thousand _____

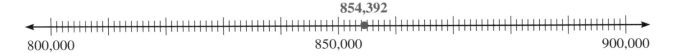

4. 627,538 to the nearest thousand _____

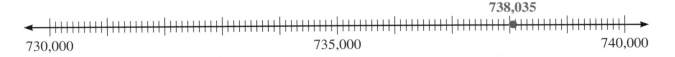

5. 89,932 to the nearest thousand _____

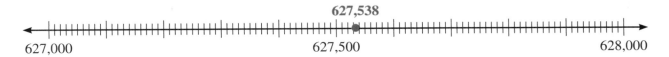

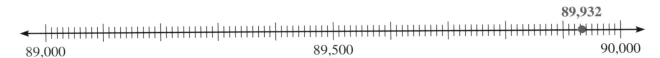

Round.

6. 243,093 to the nearest hundred thousand _____

7. 305,493 to the nearest ten thousand _____

8. 78,943 to the nearest thousand _____

9. 187,329 to the nearest hundred thousand _____

10. 96,382 to the nearest ten thousand _____

11. 249,584 to the nearest thousand _____

12. 473,986 to the nearest ten thousand _____

13. 86,394 to the nearest hundred thousand _____

14. 29,593 to the nearest thousand _____

15. 684,392 to the nearest thousand _____

Addition and Subtraction with Larger Numbers (A)

Practice Adding Multidigit Whole Numbers Up to 1 Million

Estimate the sum.

1. $31,923 + 29,384$ _____

2. $3,837 + 1,076$ _____

3. $294,204 + 313,048$ _____

4. $72,382 + 5,192$ _____

5. $382,084 + 90,371$ _____

Add

6.
$$\begin{array}{r} 2,125 \\ +\ 1,434 \\ \hline \end{array}$$

7.
$$\begin{array}{r} 18,382 \\ +\ 24,215 \\ \hline \end{array}$$

8.
$$\begin{array}{r} 382,173 \\ +\ 423,643 \\ \hline \end{array}$$

9.
$$\begin{array}{r} 4,742 \\ +\ 193 \\ \hline \end{array}$$

10. $3{,}462 + 8{,}723$ _____

11. $32{,}372 + 16{,}282$ _____

12. $129{,}701 + 262{,}712$ _____

13. $184{,}837 + 83{,}901$ _____

14. $834{,}283 + 7{,}725$ _____

Solve.

15. Kiki adds $63{,}427 + 27{,}032$ and gets $90{,}459$.

Is her solution reasonable? Explain.

_____

_____

_____

_____

_____

I wish my puppy were reasonable…

Addition and Subtraction with Larger Numbers (B)

Practice Subtracting Multidigit Whole Numbers Up to 1 Million

Estimate the difference.

1. 7,289 − 4,830 _____

2. 28,493 − 12,399 _____

3. 689,304 − 328,484 _____

4. 41,389 − 2,893 _____

5. 483,744 − 59,838 _____

6. 302,485 − 7,248 _____

Subtract.

7.
```
    5, 3 8 4
 −  2, 3 8 2
```

8.
```
    8, 0 3 7
 −  3, 4 1 2
```

9.
```
   2 8, 3 8 4
 − 1 8, 7 1 3
```

10.
```
   5 9 3, 2 6 1
 − 2 8 6, 7 2 9
```

11.

```
  6 3, 8 4 0
−    8, 2 1 9
```

12.

```
  4 2 7, 8 3 1
−    8 9, 3 2 6
```

13. 6,382 − 2,293 _____

14. 9,527 − 4,826 _____

Time to regroup!

15. 57,827 − 34,728 _____

16. 68,264 − 47,283 _____

17. 84,758 − 4,483 _____

18. 683,738 − 37,475 _____

Solve.

19. Min subtracts 7,198 − 3,073 and gets 3,125 as an answer.

Is his solution reasonable? Explain.

_____

_____

_____

_____

Addition and Subtraction with Larger Numbers (C)

Practice Adding and Subtracting Large Numbers in Problems

Answer the questions.

1. Tickets to a carnival are sold on Friday, Saturday, and Sunday. Ticket sales total $3,072 on Friday, $5,082 on Saturday, and $4,134 on Sunday.

   a. What are ticket sales for all three days combined? _____

   b. What are ticket sales for Saturday and Sunday combined? _____

   c. Let t represent how much more ticket sales are on Saturday and Sunday than on Friday. Write an equation you can use to solve for t.

   _____

   d. How much more are ticket sales on Saturday and Sunday than

   on Friday? _____

2. This table shows the number of points Sarah and Jordan score playing a video game. They each play two rounds of the game.

Points Scored		
Player	Round 1	Round 2
Sarah	8,573	7,457
Jordan	9,572	6,846

   a. How many points does Sarah score in rounds 1 and 2 combined? _____

   b. How many points does Jordan score in rounds 1 and 2 combined? _____

c. Let p represent how many more points Jordan scores than Sarah in rounds 1 and 2 combined. Write an equation you can use to solve for p.

_____

d. How many more points does Jordan score than Sarah in rounds

1 and 2 combined? _____

3. An airplane flying at an altitude of 14,382 feet ascends another 9,372 feet. A little while later, it descends 10,345 feet.

What is the altitude of the airplane after it descends? _____

4. Kiki, Min, and Sarah each sell magazines to raise money for their soccer team. Kiki raises $1,294. Min raises $1,053, and Sarah raises $1,129.

How much money do they raise altogether? _____

5. Jordan keeps track of the number of calories he eats for four days. This table shows how many calories he eats each day.

Daily Calories	
Day	Calories consumed
Monday	2,834
Tuesday	3,283
Wednesday	2,293
Thursday	2,637

How many more calories does Jordan eat on Monday and Tuesday combined than on Wednesday and Thursday combined?

_____

Multiplying and Dividing with 4-Digit Numbers (A)

Practice Multiplying 4-Digits by 1-Digit

Multiply.

1. $5 \times 1,000 =$ _____

2. $4 \times 6,000 =$ _____

Complete the area model to find the product.

3. $2,385 \times 4$

	2,000	300	80	5
4				

$2,385 \times 4 =$ _____

4. $6,750 \times 3$

	6,000	700	50
3			

$6,750 \times 3 =$ _____

5. $8,468 \times 9$

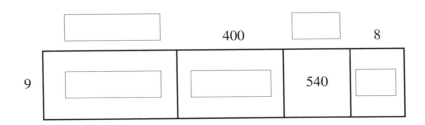

		400		8
9			540	

$8,468 \times 9 =$ _____

Multiply using equations.

6. $2{,}719 \times 6 = ($ [____] $+ 700 +$ [____] $+ 9) \times 6$

   $= $ [____] $\times 6 + 700 \times$ [____] $+$ [____] $\times 6 + 9 \times 6$

   $= $ [____] $+$ [____] $+$ [____] $+$ [____]

   $= $ [____]

Estimate the product.

7. $8{,}168 \times 9 \approx$ _____

8. $4{,}893 \times 5 \approx$ _____

Multiply.

9.
```
      2 , 3 8 2
    ×         4
    _____
    □ , □ □ □
```

10.
```
      5 , 3 8 2
    ×         3
    _____
    □ □ , □ □ □
```

11.
```
      4 , 8 3 9
    ×         7
    _____
    □ □ , □ □ □
```

12.
```
      6 , 3 8 2
    ×         5
    _____
    □ □ , □ □ □
```

13.
```
      8 , 4 7 3
    ×         6
    _____
    □ □ , □ □ □
```

14.
```
      7 , 3 8 2
    ×         4
    _____
    □ □ , □ □ □
```

Multiplying and Dividing with 4-Digit Numbers (B)

Practice Dividing Larger Numbers – No Remainders

Complete the area model to divide.

1. $8,376 \div 6$

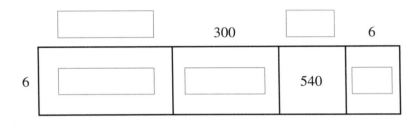

		300		6
6			540	

$8,376 \div 6 =$ _____

2. $3,213 \div 7$

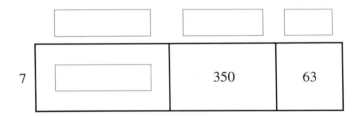

7		350	63

$3,213 \div 7 =$ _____

Complete the equations that describe the division shown in the model.

3. $8,304 \div 6$

	1,000	300	80	4
6	6,000	1,800	480	24

$8,304 \div 6 = \boxed{} \div 6 + 1,800 \div \boxed{} + 480 \div 6 + 24 \div 6$

$\qquad = \boxed{} + \boxed{} + 80 + 4$

$\qquad = \boxed{}$

Divide.

4. $4 \overline{)\ 5,184}$

5. $3 \overline{)\ 6,168}$

6. $5 \overline{)\ 3,905}$

7. $7 \overline{)\ 4,396}$

8. $6,484 \div 4$ _____

9. $6,102 \div 3$ _____

10. $5,096 \div 7$ _____

Dividing larger numbers is just like dividing smaller numbers.

11. $4,626 \div 9$ _____

Multiplying and Dividing with 4-Digit Numbers (C)

Practice Dividing Larger Numbers with Remainders

Complete the area model to divide.

1.

				7

5		1,500		35		

$6,988 \div 5 = $ _____ R _____

2.

4			12		

$2,374 \div 4 = $ _____ R _____

I have to think a little harder when a division problem has a remainder.

Divide.

3. $3 \overline{)\ 5,285}$ ⬜ R ⬜

4. $4 \overline{)\ 9,547}$ ⬜ R ⬜

5. $5 \overline{)\ 4,786}$ ⬜ R ⬜

6. $5 \overline{)\ 9,519}$ ⬜ R ⬜

7. $6{,}953 \div 3$ _____ R _____

8. $2{,}318 \div 8$ _____ R _____

9. $6{,}413 \div 4$ _____ R _____

10. $3{,}670 \div 9$ _____ R _____

Multiplying and Dividing with 4-Digit Numbers (D)

Practice Solving Problems Involving Larger Numbers

Answer the questions.

1. Maria travels 1,820 miles in 4 days. She travels the same number of miles each day.

   How many miles does she travel each day? _____

2. Jada and Juan play a video game. Juan scores 3,696 points. His score is 4 times the number of points that Jada scores.

   How many points does Jada score? _____

3. James participates in a fundraiser that raises $5,320. The money is divided evenly among 5 different charities.

   How much money does each charity receive? _____

4. A factory produces 3,117 cans of soup. The cans are packaged in boxes. Each box holds 8 cans of soup.

   a. How many boxes are filled with cans? _____

   b. How many cans are left over? _____

5. One night, 1,444 people attend a concert. Six sections of seating are provided for the attendees. Each section has the same number of seats.

   a. How many people could be seated in each section? _____

   b. How many people could **not** be seated? _____

6. Tickets are sold for a play. This table shows how many adult and child tickets are sold. An adult ticket costs $8. A child ticket costs $5.

Ticket type	Number sold
adult	1,012
child	683

a. How much money is collected in adult ticket sales? _____

b. How much money is collected in child ticket sales? _____

c. What is the total amount of money collected in all ticket sales? _____

7. A meal is made up of chicken, rice, and steamed vegetables. This table shows the number of calories each food adds to the meal.

Food	Total calories
chicken	1,720
rice	1,648
steamed vegetables	400

The meal serves 8 people. How many calories are in each serving? _____

8. Amelie's older sister has two jobs. In 8 months, she earns $1,880 in her first job and $1,024 in her second job. She earns that same amount of money each month.

How much money does Amelie's older sister earn each month? _____

Parallel and Perpendicular Lines (A)

Practice Drawing Parallel and Perpendicular Lines

Follow the steps to draw the figure.

1. Draw two lines that are parallel.

   a. Use a ruler to draw a straight line.

   b. Use the ruler to make a point on one side of the line.

   How far is the point from the line?

   _____

   c. Move the ruler and mark a second point on the same side of the line. Use the same distance as the first point.

   d. Draw a line through the two points.

2. Draw two lines that intersect but are **not** perpendicular.

   a. Use a ruler to draw a straight line.

   b. Rotate the ruler slightly and draw a second line. Make sure this line intersects the first line without making a right angle.

3. Draw two lines that are perpendicular.

    a. Use a ruler to draw a straight line.

    b. Draw a point anywhere on the line.

    c. Use the protractor to mark a 90° angle from the point. To do this, place the origin of the protractor on the point. Align the baseline of the protractor with the line. Locate 90° on the protractor and draw a point.

    d. Draw a line through the two points.

Determine whether the statement is True or False.

4. Parallel lines never cross. _____

5. Perpendicular lines intersect at right angles. _____

6. Parallel lines are lines that intersect. _____

7. Perpendicular lines form acute and obtuse angles. _____

8. Parallel lines are always the same distance apart. _____

9. Perpendicular lines never cross. _____

Draw a line parallel to the given line.

10.

11.

12.

13.

When I was picking these apples, I noticed that the trees were parallel to each other.

Draw a line perpendicular to the given line.

14.

15.

16.

17.

Parallel and Perpendicular Lines (B)

Practice: Working with 2-Dimensional Figures

Answer the question about the figures.

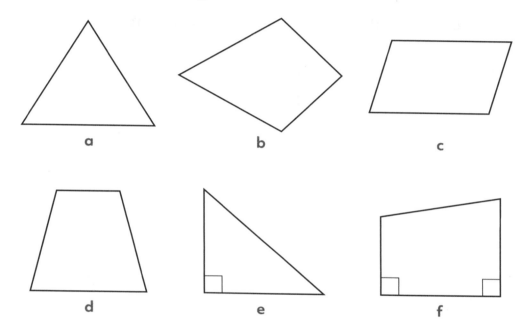

1. Which shapes have parallel lines? _____

2. Which shapes have perpendicular lines? _____

3. Which shapes do **not** have parallel *or* perpendicular lines? _____

Fill in the blanks.

4. This shape is a trapezoid.

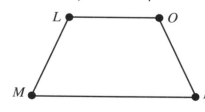

Line segment _____ is parallel

to line segment _____ .

5. This shape is a rectangle.

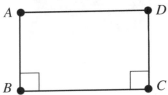

a. Line segment *AD* is perpendicular to line segment

_____ and line segment _____ .

b. Line segment *AD* is parallel to line segment _____ .

Write the names of the points, lines, line segments, and rays shown in the figure.

6.

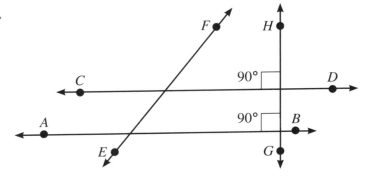

a. 3 points: _____ _____ _____

b. 2 line segments: _____ _____

c. 3 lines: _____ _____ _____

d. 2 rays: _____ _____

e. 2 parallel lines: _____ is parallel to _____ .

f. 2 perpendicular lines: _____ is perpendicular to _____ .

g. 2 lines that intersect but are **not** perpendicular: _____ intersects

_____ .

Parallel and Perpendicular Lines (C)

Practice Classifying Shapes by Line Pairs

Use the terms from the word bank to answer the question. Terms can be used more than once.

right triangle	square	rectangle	quadrilateral
parallelogram	rhombus	trapezoid	

1. Which shapes **always** have perpendicular lines?

   _____

2. Which shapes could—but do **not** always—have perpendicular lines?

   _____

3. Which shape **always** has exactly 1 pair of parallel lines? _____

4. Which shapes have 2 pairs of parallel lines?

   _____

5. Which terms could be used to classify this shape?

   _____ and _____

6. Which terms could be used to classify this shape?

_____ and _____

Answer the question.

7. Can a pentagon or a hexagon have parallel or perpendicular sides?

   Explain your answer using words or a sketch. _____

8. Can a triangle have parallel sides? Explain your answer using words or a sketch.

   _____

   _____

9. Could this shape be a trapezoid? Explain.

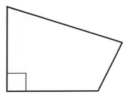

   _____

   _____

Draw the figures, and then answer the question.

10. Use a ruler to draw a parallelogram and a trapezoid. Explain how these two shapes are alike and how they are different.

_____

_____

_____

_____

11. Use a ruler to draw a rhombus that doesn't have perpendicular sides and a square. Explain how these two shapes are alike and how they are different.

_____

_____

_____

_____

Describe the characteristics of the shape.

12. parallelogram

_____

_____

_____

_____

13. trapezoid

_____

_____

_____

_____

14. rectangle

_____

_____

_____

_____

Looking at shapes can be very relaxing.

Classifying Shapes (A)

Practice Identifying Angles in 2-Dimensional Shapes

Fill in the blanks to complete the statement.

1. The measure of an acute angle is between _____ and _____.

2. The measure of a right angle is exactly _____.

3. The measure of an obtuse angle is between _____ and _____.

Label each angle in the figure as acute, right, or obtuse. Then, fill in the blanks to complete the statement.

4.

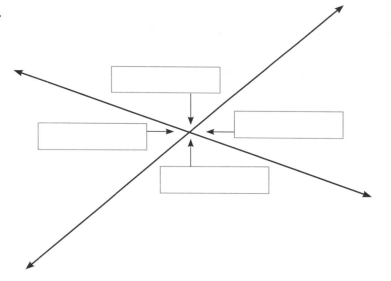

There are _____ acute angles, _____ right angles, and

_____ obtuse angles in this figure.

5.

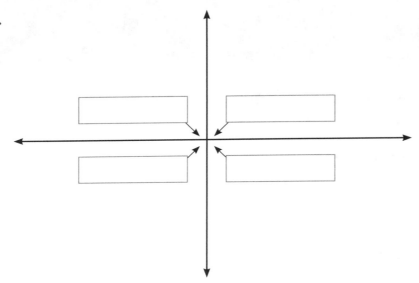

There are _____ acute angles, _____ right angles, and

_____ obtuse angles in this figure.

Fill in the blanks. Classify each angle as acute, right, or obtuse.

6.

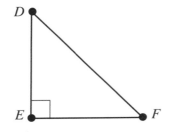

Angle *D* is _____, angle *E* is _____,

and angle *F* is _____.

7.

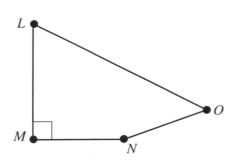

Angle *L* is _____, angle *M* is _____,

angle *N* is _____, and angle *O* is _____.

Practice Classifying Shapes

Use the terms from the word bank to answer the question.
Terms can be used more than once or not at all.

rectangle	quadrilateral	square
acute triangle	right triangle	obtuse triangle

1. Which shapes **always** have 4 right angles? _____

2. Which shapes **always** have at least 2 acute angles? _____

    _____

3. Which shape **always** has 3 acute angles? _____

4. Which shape **always** has exactly 1 right angle? _____

5. Which shape **always** has exactly 1 obtuse angle? _____

Classify the triangle as right, obtuse, or acute.

6.

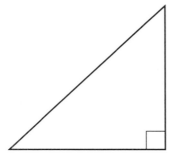

7.

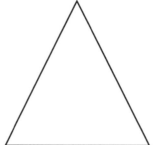

8.

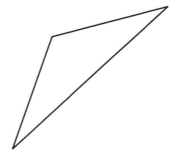

9.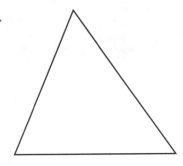

10.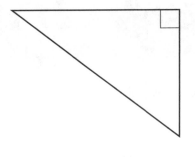

11.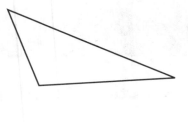

_____   _____   _____

Identify the shape, and then answer the question.

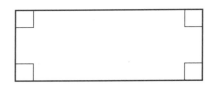         

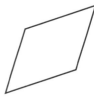   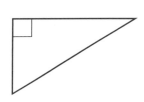   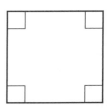   

12. Circle the square. Explain how you know this shape is a square.

_____

_____

13. Shade the rectangle. Explain how you know this shape is a rectangle.

_____

_____

Symmetry (A)

Practice Exploring Symmetry

Answer the question.

1. What is a line of symmetry?

    _____

    _____

    _____

2. How can you determine whether a line across an image is a line of symmetry?

    _____

    _____

    _____

3. Kiki examines this figure. She decides that both lines are lines of symmetry.

    Is Kiki correct? Explain your answer.

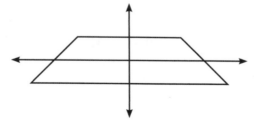

    _____

    _____

Determine whether the dashed line is a line of symmetry. Write Yes or No.

4.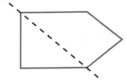

_____

5.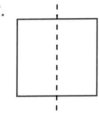

_____

6.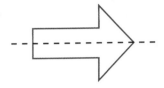

_____

7.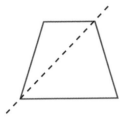

_____

8.

_____

9.

_____

10.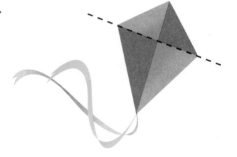

_____

11.

_____

Practice Working with Lines of Symmetry

Answer the question.

1. Min determines that this quadrilateral has no lines of symmetry.

   Is Min correct? Explain.

   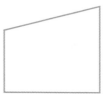

   _____

   _____

2. Kiki determines that this figure has at least 1 line of symmetry.

   Is Kiki correct? Explain.

   _____

   _____

Circle the answers.

3. Which pictures have at least 1 line of symmetry?

   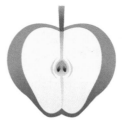

4. Which letters have at least 1 line of symmetry?

 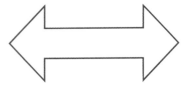  

5. Which shapes have at least 1 line of symmetry?

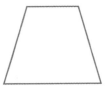 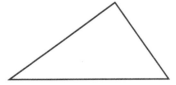

Draw a line or lines of symmetry on the shape.

6. 1 line of symmetry

7. 1 line of symmetry

8. 2 lines of symmetry

9. 4 lines of symmetry

Glossary

acute angle – an angle that measures greater than 0° and less than 90°

acute triangle – a triangle with three acute angles

algorithm – a step-by-step way to solve a problem

area – the amount of space on a flat surface, most often measured in square units

area model – a model for multiplication that shows the product of two factors as the total number of squares on a rectangular grid; one factor is the number of rows and the other factor is the number of columns

array – a pattern of objects or numbers placed in a rectangular formation of rows and columns

base – the number repeatedly multiplied when the number has an exponent

benchmark number – a number that can be used to compare or estimate other numbers; whole numbers and halves are common benchmark numbers

centimeter (cm) – a metric unit used to measure length; 1 centimeter $= \frac{1}{100}$ of a meter

compatible numbers – numbers that are easy to compute using mental math

composite number – a whole number greater than 1 that is not prime

composite solid – a solid composed, or made up, of more than one solid

coordinate (on a number line) – the number associated with a point on a number line

coordinate (on the coordinate plane) – a location on the coordinate plane, designated by an x-value and a y-value

coordinate plane – a plane on which points can be located that has an x-axis and a y-axis perpendicular to each other

cubed – the result of the operation where a number has been multiplied by itself two times, such as 5 cubed $= 5^3 = 5 \times 5 \times 5 = 125$; when the volume of a cube is found, the dimensions are cubed, and the volume is expressed in units cubed

cubic centimeter – a cube that is 1 cm on each side; a measure of volume

cubic foot – a cube that is 1 ft on each side; a measure of volume

cubic inch – a cube that is 1 in. on each side; a measure of volume

cubic unit – a cube that is 1 unit on each side; a measure of volume

cup (c) – a unit for measuring capacity in the English system of measurement; 1 c $=$ 8 fl oz

data – numerical information that has been gathered

decimal number – a number written with a decimal point; sometimes called a decimal fraction

decimal place value – one of the place values that follow the decimal point in a number, such as tenths or thousandths

decimal point – the point in a decimal number that separates a whole number from the decimal (or fraction) part

degree – a unit used to measure angles

denominator – the number in a fraction that is below the fraction bar

difference – the answer to a subtraction problem

dividend – the number to be divided; the dividend divided by the divisor equals the quotient

divisor – the number that divides the dividend; the dividend divided by the divisor equals the quotient

equilateral triangle – a triangle that has all sides equal in length

equivalent fractions – fractions that name the same amount, such as $\frac{1}{2}$ and $\frac{3}{6}$

equivalent triangle – a triangle that has all sides equal in length

estimate (v.) – to make a very good guess or rough calculation of an answer when the exact answer is not necessary

evaluate – to find the value of an expression

expanded form – a way to write a number that shows the place value of each of its digits; for example, $543 = 500 + 40 + 3$ or 5 hundreds + 4 tens + 3 ones

exponent – the number of times a base number is multiplied by itself

expression – one or more numbers and symbols that show a certain value, such as $2 + 3$, or $3 \times ?$, or $10 - 4 + 1$

factor – one of two or more numbers that are multiplied

factor pairs – two numbers that multiply to give a particular product; factor pairs of 6 are 6×1 and 3×2

foot (ft) – the English, or customary, unit for measuring length that equals 12 in.

fraction – a number that represents a part of a whole or a part of a set

gallon (gal) – the English, or customary, unit for measuring capacity that equals 128 fl oz or 4 qt

gram (g) – the basic metric unit of mass

greater-than symbol (>) – a symbol that shows that one amount is greater than another

greatest common factor (GCF) – the greatest whole number that is a factor of two or more given whole numbers

grouping symbols – symbols used to set numbers or expressions apart, such as parentheses

hexagon – a 6-sided polygon

hour (h) – the unit for measuring time that equals 60 min

hundredths – the place value immediately to the right of the tenths place; 10 thousandths = 1 hundredth and 10 hundredths = 1 tenth

improper fraction – a fraction whose numerator is greater than or equal to its denominator

inch (in.) – the basic English, or customary, unit for measuring length

intersecting lines – lines that cross at one point or at all points

inverse operations – opposite operations that undo each other; subtraction and addition are inverse operations; division and multiplication are inverse operations

inverse relationship – the relationship between operations that reverse or undo each other; addition and subtraction have an inverse relationship; multiplication and division have an inverse relationship

isosceles triangle – a triangle that has at least 2 sides equal in length; an equilateral triangle is a special type of isosceles triangle

kilogram (kg) – the metric unit for measuring mass that equals 1,000 g

kilometer (km) – the metric unit for measuring distance that equals 1,000 m

least common denominator (LCD) – the least common multiple of two or more denominators

least common multiple (LCM) – the least number, other than 0, that is a multiple of two or more given whole numbers; used for the least common denominator

less-than symbol (<) – a symbol that shows that one amount is less than another

like denominators – denominators that are exactly the same in two or more fractions

line – a straight path of points that goes on forever in both directions

line plot – number line that shows all the pieces of data with a mark or marks above each piece of data to show how many times that piece of data occurred

line segment – a straight path of points that has endpoints at both ends; also called a segment

line symmetry – a type of symmetry where a plane figure can have a line or lines drawn through it so that one half is the mirror image of the other half; when the figure is folded along a line of symmetry, one half must fit exactly onto the other half

liter (L) – the basic metric unit of volume; 1 L = 1,000 mL

mass – the amount of matter in an object; the amount of mass remains the same no matter where the object is, but the weight of an object can change depending on the pull of gravity on the object

meter (m) – the basic metric unit for measuring length

milliliter (mL) – the metric unit for measuring capacity that equals $\frac{1}{1,000}$ L

minute (min) – the unit for measuring time that equals 60 s

mixed number – a whole number and a proper fraction that show a single amount

multiple – the product of a given number and any whole number

multiplication fact family – a set of four related multiplication and division facts that use the same set of three numbers

numerator – the number in a fraction that is above the fraction bar

obtuse angle – an angle that measures greater than 90° and less than 180°

obtuse triangle – a triangle with one angle greater than 90°

order of operations – a set of rules that tells the correct order to use to solve a problem that has more than one operation

ordered pair – a pair of numbers that names the location of a point

origin – the coordinate (0, 0) on a coordinate plane

ounce (oz) – the basic English, or customary, unit for measuring weight as $\frac{1}{16}$ lb and capacity as $\frac{1}{8}$ c

parallel lines – lines in the same flat surface that never intersect

parallelogram – a quadrilateral with two pairs of parallel sides

partial product – the product of each place value when a multidigit factor is multiplied by a single-digit or multidigit factor; the sum of the partial products is the final product for the problem

pentagon – a 5-sided polygon

perimeter – the distance around the edge of a shape

perpendicular lines – lines that intersect and form angles that measure 90°

pint (pt) – the English, or customary, unit for measuring capacity that equals 16 fl oz or 2 c

place value – the value of a digit depending on its position, or place, in a number

place-value chart – a chart that shows the value of each digit in a number

point – a location in space

polygon – a plane shape made of 3 or more straight sides that separate the inside of the shape from the outside

pound (lb) – the English, or customary, unit for measuring weight that equals 16 oz

power – a product in which all the factors are the same; for example, 16 is the fourth power of 2, because $2 \times 2 \times 2 \times 2 = 16$

power of 10 – a number that can be written as a power with a base of 10

prime factorization – an expression showing a whole number as a product of its prime factors

prime number – a whole number greater than 1 that has only two whole-number factors, 1 and itself

product – the answer to a multiplication problem

proper fraction – a fraction in which the numerator is less than the denominator

protractor – a tool to measure the degrees in an angle

quadrilateral – a polygon with four sides

quart (qt) – the English, or customary, unit for measuring capacity that equals 32 fl oz or 2 pt

quotient – the answer to a division problem; the dividend divided by the divisor equals the quotient

ray – a straight path of points that has an endpoint at one end and goes on forever from that endpoint

reciprocal – two numbers whose product is 1

rectangle – a parallelogram with four 90° angles; a square is a special type of rectangle

rectangular prism – a solid figure with six faces that are rectangles

reflex angle – an angle that measures greater than 180° and less than 360°

remainder – the amount left over after dividing evenly

rhombus (plural: rhombuses) – a parallelogram that has all sides equal in length; a square is a special type of rhombus

right angle – an angle that measures exactly 90°

right triangle – a triangle with a right angle

round (v.) – to change a number to the nearest place value asked in a problem; for example, rounding 532 to the nearest ten would be 530

scalene triangle – a triangle that has no sides equal in length

second – the basic unit for measuring time

simplest form – of fractions, a fraction with a numerator and denominator that have no common factor other than 1

solid figure – a figure with three dimensions: length, width, and height or depth

square – a parallelogram that has all sides equal in length and four 90° angles

standard form – the usual way of writing a number using digits

straight angle – an angle that measures exactly 180°; a straight angle is a line

tenths – the place value immediately to the right of the ones place after the decimal; 10 hundredths = 1 tenth and 10 tenths = 1

term in a pattern – each number or object in a pattern

thousandths – the place value immediately to the right of the hundredths place after the decimal; 10 thousandths = 1 hundredth

ton – the English, or customary, unit for measuring weight that equals 2,000 lb

trapezoid – a quadrilateral with exactly one pair of parallel sides

triangle – a polygon with three sides

unit fraction – a fraction with a numerator of 1, such as $\frac{1}{3}$ or $\frac{1}{7}$

unlike denominators – denominators that are different in two or more fractions

vertex (plural: vertices) – the common endpoint of two rays that form an angle

volume – the amount of space taken up by a three-dimensional object; measured in cubic units

weight – the measure of how heavy an object is, such as 10 lb

whole numbers – zero and the counting numbers (0, 1, 2, 3, 4, 5, 6, and so on)

x-axis – the horizontal axis on a coordinate plane, perpendicular to the y-axis

x-coordinate – the first value in an ordered pair, such as 5 in the ordered pair (5, 6)

y-axis – the vertical axis on a coordinate plane, perpendicular to the x-axis

y-coordinate – the second value in an ordered pair, such as 6 in the ordered pair (5, 6)

yard (yd) – the English, or customary, unit for measuring length that equals 36 in. or 3 ft

Data Sources

Unit 5 Adding and Subtracting Fractions and Mixed Numbers

AKC (American Kennel Club) Staff. "Breed weight chart," May 11, 2017. Accessed May 2, 2018. https://www.akc.org/expert-advice/nutrition/weight-management/breed-weight-chart/

Unit 9 Division by a 1-Digit Divisor with Remainders

PlantMaps. "Florida Record High and Low Temperatures Map." Accessed August 19, 2018. https://www.plantmaps.com/florida-record-high-and-low-temperature-map.php

Unit 12 Problem Solving Involving Measurements

AKC (American Kennel Club) Staff. "Breed weight chart," May 11, 2017. Accessed August 28, 2018. https://www.akc.org/expert-advice/nutrition/weight-management/breed-weight-chart/

National Park Service. "Bandelier National Monument New Mexico – Identification of Common Butterflies," February 24, 2015. Accessed August 28, 2018. https://www.nps.gov/band/learn/nature/id-of-common-butterflies.htm